EVERYDAY HOCKEY HEROES

VOLUME III

MORE UPLIFTING STORIES CELEBRATING OUR GREAT GAME

JIM LANG

Published by Simon & Schuster
NEW YORK   LONDON   TORONTO   SYDNEY   NEW DELHI

SIMON &
SCHUSTER
CANADA

A Division of Simon & Schuster, LLC
166 King Street East, Suite 300
Toronto, Ontario M5A 1J3

This Simon & Schuster Canada edition November 2024

SIMON & SCHUSTER CANADA and colophon are trademarks of Simon & Schuster, LLC

Simon & Schuster: Celebrating 100 Years of Publishing in 2024

For information about special discounts for bulk purchases,
please contact Simon & Schuster Special Sales at 1-800-268-3216
or CustomerService@simonandschuster.ca.

Manufactured in the United States of America

1   3   5   7   9   10   8   6   4   2

Library and Archives Canada Cataloguing in Publication

Title: Everyday hockey heroes. Volume III : more uplifting stories
celebrating our great game / Jim Lang
Names: Lang, Jim, 1965– author. | McKenzie, Bob. Everyday hockey heroes.
Description: Simon & Schuster Canada edition. | Previous volumes
authored by Bob McKenzie & Jim Lang.
Identifiers: Canadiana (print) 20220186863 | Canadiana (ebook) 2022018691X |
ISBN 9781982196547 (softcover) | ISBN 9781982196561 (EPUB)
Subjects: LCSH: Hockey—Canada—Biography. | LCSH: Hockey—Canada. |
LCSH: Hockey—Anecdotes. | LCGFT: Biographies. | LCGFT: Anecdotes.
Classification: LCC GV848.5.A1 L36 2024 | DDC 796.962092/2—dc23

ISBN 978-1-9821-9654-7
ISBN 978-1-9821-9656-1 (ebook)

IMAGE CREDITS: All images provided by the subjects, except for the following:

Jason Payne: Tony Bailey Photography
Kelly Serbu: kelly clark fotography
Kim McCullough: Sasha Kasumi Kobo—Kaptured by Kobo

To all the heroes who make hockey a better game

Contents

Foreword

I guess we could start with the question "What is the game of hockey?" To many of us, I suppose the game of hockey is the sport which we are most passionate about. From growing up watching *Hockey Night in Canada* to the outdoor rinks, to the camaraderie of the locker room, on to the rigors of competitive hockey at all levels and even for some the lifetime dream of suiting up in the National Hockey League, is there a greater purpose around the game than just that of the game itself?

Upon the completion of my playing career, I had the honour of coaching youth hockey in suburban Philadelphia, on the New Jersey side of the river, where we stayed upon my retirement. I coached for several reasons: to give back to the game I love, to coach my own boys on the joys of the sport, and to teach aspiring athletes who had a similar love for the game how to compete hard, how to win with humility, and how to lose gracefully.

All these reasons gave me purpose, and I relished the anonymity that it afforded me except with those who I was coaching. And I truly believed my role in life and the mark I wanted to make on them wasn't entirely about the game but more importantly the life of hockey. Even though each of these players aspired to play at the highest level, the reality was their dreams might not be achieved. But what the game could give to them was an understanding about how to have an impact on the lives of others, whether through their actions, philanthropy, the discipline of an educated skill set, or just general acts of kindness. The sport affords all of us at least one common thread. An ability to give back. There is a higher calling for our sport. I am often asked why professional hockey players are the best athletes regarding the fans and giving back. I have a theory. The theory goes that our parents sacrificed and gave us what we so desperately wanted: to play the game of hockey. That comes with a price, both from a time commitment and financial perspective. Their sacrifices and commitment to our dreams and aspirations are remarkable, commendable, and inspirational. Thus, we have no justification or excuse not to share our knowledge, wisdom, and mentality by paying it forward.

Although my career ended due to postconcussion, I have never felt cheated by the game. I played fifteen years professionally, got to coach my boys through their childhood, then continued to watch them as they followed their different paths to where they are today. It was never easy, but the sport gave me so many greater things to be excited and proud of. I believe in my soul that this is the case for so many of us who view the game as a microcosm of our lives and the service it can be to others.

The game of hockey is amazing, especially today's game with the skill and speed and athleticism of athletes, but the sport has never been only about the speed and skill; it is also about the human connection and the humanity that is inspired in so many of us to give back in different ways and to tell our story as seen through our eyes. The stories compiled here tell a tale of so much more than just the game of hockey.

Keith Primeau
May 2024

Introduction

In the Merriam-Webster dictionary, a hero is defined as a person who is the object of extreme or uncritical devotion.

Someone defined as an Everyday Hockey Hero doesn't quite fit that definition. The Everyday Hockey Hero is someone who exceeds all expectations to make hockey a better sport, usually without receiving any recognition. They didn't set out to receive any of the recognition that might have come their way. Far from it. This is a group of impressive individuals who quietly go about their business, working hard to improve hockey in their own way.

This is the third time I have had the privilege of working on an *Everyday Hockey Heroes* book. Like the previous two times, I came away a better person. And I learned something about hockey, and about life, that I never knew before.

I was fascinated to learn more about Angela James, Mark Borowiecki, Dean Barnes, Graham McWaters, Michelle Reid and her family, Jason Payne, blind hockey player Kelly Serbu, Rob Kerr, Leonard Lye, Jim Paek, Marian Jacko, the women of Windsor who are trying to make a difference through hockey, respected journalist Sunaya Sapurji, Kim McCullough, and last, but certainly not least, the Boulet family. The people in this book are as diverse a group of individuals as you will find. But thanks to hockey, they are all connected to each other in their own unique way. They are all making hockey a better sport. And after speaking with them and learning about their stories, they made me a better person once again.

Writing this book with them reminded me of something Rod Brind'Amour said to me and the other reporters who were asking him questions between game 1 and game 2 of the 2006 Stanley Cup Final. "You don't know what you don't know." The older I get, the more I realize that Brind'Amour was so right. We go about life and think we know so much, but when we really speak to someone, and get to know their personal stories, we quickly realize how little we know.

This book was a journey that started a number of years ago and took time to put together. But once you read the stories within, you will realize that it was well worth the wait.

Jim Lang
March 2024

EVERYDAY
HOCKEY
HEROES

VOLUME III

The First Great Star

Angela James

I stood in front of the crowd gathered at the Hockey Hall of Fame for the induction ceremony, looking out at all the faces, and wondered how I would get through my speech.

It was November 8, 2010, and I, along with Cammi Granato, was being inducted. We were the first women, and I was the first Black woman. It was a surreal moment. I couldn't help but think, *Should I really be here?* I didn't think I belonged. But there my face was, enshrined in the Grand Hall. It took a while for it all to sink in because, growing up in the housing projects of Toronto in the seventies, I had faced a lot of challenges. But it was hockey that showed me what life could be beyond the rough part of the city where I grew up.

I was just over a year old when we moved to Flemingdon Park in North York. It's an area known as a working-class neighbourhood, with a number of high-rise apartment and office buildings with more than twenty thousand people calling it home. My mother, who was raising five kids on her own, had secured subsidized housing there. I can still remember the day we moved into the townhouse. I was sitting on a box, and all around me everyone was moving things into our apartment, but my focus was on this hole in the pavement of the underground garage. I later found out this hole was where everyone put their garbage for weekly pickup. For me, though, it was a hockey net.

All the neighbourhood kids played ball hockey there, and I was no different. From the time I was in kindergarten, I played hockey. Occasionally, our games would end up in the streets, but if it was raining or snowing, the underground garage was my spot. We didn't have a car, and neither did many other people, so the place was spacious, but I always kept track of when our next-door neighbour was gone with his car because there was even more room to play.

Eventually, I taught myself how to skate. Flemingdon Park had an outdoor arena, and in the winter, when the ice was in, there was one man who was hearing-impaired who was often out on the rink. I would watch how he moved across the ice and then mimic his skating.

Life was fairly simple. I would go to school. We had an outdoor community pool for swimming, which I enjoyed. Sometimes we would shoplift milk at the Dominion grocery store. To me, Flemingdon Park was my whole world. It wasn't until later that I realized there was a life beyond the park, and hockey made that possible.

But living in Flemingdon Park also came with challenges. At that time, it was a tough neighbourhood. Everybody who lived there was poor. Everybody relied on government agencies for the basic necessities. As a result, people did what they needed to survive and make ends meet. We had drug dealers, we had prostitutes, we had pimps, and there were stories that people were running after-hours clubs from their homes. Even after saying all that, I wouldn't change a thing from my childhood. It is what made me who I am today, and it made me understand what I had to overcome to get where I am today. It isn't always about just money that makes people happy. Sometimes, it is the community that matters. And despite all of the obstacles he had to overcome, we had a really good community back then.

But as a kid, it was easy to get into trouble. Depending on the day, I could find myself having a lot of fun with my friends, but other days, I found myself getting into a lot of fights. Sometimes, I would get into a fistfight just to get to school. In Flemingdon, everyone wanted to be the strongest, and fighting was what we had to do to survive.

As for being a girl who played hockey, it was instilled in me from an early age that if I wanted to win, I'd have to fight for it.

One day when I was seven or eight, I was playing a game of pickup hockey when one of the men watching came up to my mom and said, "You need to get Angela involved in organized hockey because she can really play." I don't know who he was, but I owe him a thank-you because my mom listened to his advice. In the seventies, there were very few organized girls hockey leagues, so my mom enrolled me in the Flemingdon boys league. I started at the novice level, at seven years old. At times, my mom worked various jobs. But for the most part growing up, she worked the one job and relied on the government housing subsidy. Hockey back then was so different. To get to hockey back then when I was a kid, I would take the bus, or other times, another parent would take me.

At first, the league didn't want to include me because I was a girl and only did after my mom threatened legal action. But soon I was moved up to Atom, and then the Pee Wee league because they were impressed with my skills. I guess I was good, but all I knew for certain was that I loved to play.

After two years with the boys league, the organization decided to change their rules to prohibit girls from playing alongside boys. I was devastated. Once again, my mom fought to get them to allow me to continue playing, but this time it was no use.

Now I know that the organization was sexist, but at the time I couldn't understand why I wasn't allowed to play. I saw girls playing hockey around Flemingdon Park. I remember standing on my tiptoes, my chin on the board, and thinking, *These girls look pretty good. I guess girls really do play hockey.* But I wondered how a girl would ever be able to play competitively, beyond a pickup game.

It was around this time that I went through a rough patch at school. I was getting into so much trouble that in grade four, I got kicked out. The school board sent me to an all-girls school that was run by nuns, but after one day there, I never went back. I just stayed at the local dairy-mart. When the board realized the all-girls school wasn't working, they let me go back to my old school.

Things changed when I entered Valley Park Junior High in grade seven. The vice principal at the school was a strict man named Ross Dixon. Mr. Dixon handled all the troubled kids at school, and he had a big influence on me. He made me see that there was more to life than hanging out at the park, getting into trouble, and playing sports. He was a positive authority figure for me at an important time in my life.

He was a stickler for rules at school. Growing up, we didn't have a lot of rules. He was one of the first people to introduce a set of rules to me. He also taught the importance of common sense and let me believe that I could do it. He convinced me that academics would mean something in my life one day.

Growing up, I didn't have a strong male figure to look up to. I knew of my father, but he wasn't in my life, so having someone like Mr. Dixon was good for me. And thanks to his guidance, I turned things around at school and improved my grades.

Hockey also helped me go in the right direction. After I was kicked out of the Flemingdon boys league, my mom found a new girls hockey league that had just started in nearby Don Mills. The day I showed up, I was shocked to see a lot of the girls were still in figure skates, but after a while, I hit my stride. I had so many cool memories when I started playing girls hockey. Playing with girls that were older with me, that is where I learned how to drink! The main thing that kept me grounded and staying out of trouble was playing a lot of hockey. I loved going away on tournaments and having fun with the girls and the parents. I loved the competition and visiting some of those classic old rinks across Ontario.

When I was playing Pee Wee hockey on the boys team, that was when we went to the tournament in Lachine, Quebec. Then, when I was fourteen years old and playing on the girls team, we would travel to Picton, Ontario, for their big tournament. We always looked forward to the yearly tournament in Brampton. All the tournaments and all the travel, that was the highlight of playing hockey back then. If we were lucky, there were times we stayed at places with a swimming pool. But usually, we stayed in motels.

My mom was working all the time, so getting to all my games was a challenge. Fortunately, my older sister, Kim, taught me how to use the TTC transit system. She was good at navigating around the city and would often take me to my games, and whenever she couldn't, she would make sure I got on the right bus. As I moved up in the league and got to know my teammates, I started to get rides with the other players.

I was recruited by Seneca College while I was playing softball in the senior league. A woman by the name of Mary Zetel, who has since passed on, was the reason I ended up at Seneca. If it wasn't for her, I never would have gone there. Before she recruited me, I wasn't even thinking of post-secondary education. Mary's place was near the ball diamond. We were there after a game, and everyone was having a beer. And I was having a beer with them. She walked by us and looked at me and said, "How old are you?"

I told her that I was almost sixteen.

She looked at me and said, "Well, why are you drinking?" I looked at her and said, "Because I'm thirsty."

We started talking, and then she asked me if I was thinking of college. At the time, I had been recruited to go to Northeastern University in Boston. I had gone down there to visit the campus. I realized that I would have been too homesick and so that never worked out.

In my time at Seneca, I led the league in scoring and was named MVP three seasons in a row. My final year was my best showing—I scored 50 goals in 14 games. I always joke that I scored all those goals because of my Graf skates. There were my good-luck skates. They had a bit of a forward tilt. I used to fall on my face quite a bit, but I was able to score a lot of goals with them.

This was when women's hockey in Canada really began to improve. Not only was it being recognized, but the game itself was improving, and I benefited from playing in a league full of talented players who had fought for the chance to be there, just like me.

In 1982, they held the first national championships for women's hockey in Canada, in Brantford, Ontario, the home of Wayne Gretzky. I was barely seventeen years old at the time, and I got to play for Team Ontario. I'd gone from not even having a league to play in as a child to representing my whole province with a team of great women players.

During that time, if you played women's hockey, the big show was playing for your province in the nationals, and the competition got better every year, because only the best were chosen to represent their province. The hockey became more organized, the quality improved, and we were receiving better coaching and more ice time, and even sponsorships.

It was a lot of pressure for a sixteen-year-old, and I was young compared to the other players. I was playing in the Canadian Women's Hockey League (CWHL) when I was barely sixteen. That wasn't always the greatest, but being that young in such a competitive league made me work harder. And my mom entrusted a couple of the older girls to look after me. They made sure I didn't get into any trouble. One of them was a woman named Anne; she was my mentor and took me under her wing. Anne knew that I was young, and she was older and had a vehicle. She was from a well-to-do family and my mother trusted her to keep an eye on me. As much as my mom couldn't do everything for me, she always made sure that I got everything that I needed.

Hockey is a team sport. As much as I would like to stay out there the whole game, that is impossible. While I put up good numbers, I always had a lot of help from my teammates. And I was always trying to learn from the people around me. While I was playing for Seneca College, some of the other colleges had some really talented players.

While I excelled at hockey, it took me longer before I began to excel at academics. My first year at Seneca, I was a horrible student. I partied all the time and I ended up on academic probation. The school set me up with a tutor, and after that I got serious about doing my homework. I was a decent student in high school. The next year, I ended up on the honour roll, and by the end, I excelled in my academics. While I was going to Seneca and playing varsity hockey for the school, I also played senior hockey on the side. On top of that, I was working as well. I had a lot on my plate at the time.

I was a busgirl at the Ponderosa Steakhouse, then I worked as a busgirl at a restaurant at the local Holiday Inn. I also started to work as a referee, and I ended up officiating intramural hockey games while I was going to Seneca. Then I had a job at a restaurant in downtown Toronto that wouldn't end until one in the morning. It was at a place Ginsberg & Wong. I worked there for a few years, but after a while, it was too much to work there and get up for school in the morning, so I left.

Between playing in the CWHL and playing at Seneca College, my game continually improved. As I got into my late teens and early twenties, I started to receive a little respect for my game and my achievements. The Ontario Colleges Athletic Association (OCAA) named me their athlete of the year in 1984 and 1985, partly because of the scoring records. It was such a shame when, in 1989, the OCAA ended its women's hockey program. The issue? Too few competing teams to keep it going.

I played at the highest level of women's hockey in Canada for years, moving to senior hockey and playing for different teams as leagues came and went, and the competition moved from place to place. I went to the national championships twelve times, and it all culminated with one of my proudest moments: playing for Team Canada in the first official IIHF Women's World Championship in 1990. It was held in Ottawa, and we took home the gold medal.

In 1990, they came up with this Pink Power marketing campaign.

There was pink everywhere, they even had pink flamingoes on the Zamboni. They spray-painted our sticks black, and at the same time, we were all wearing white Tackla hockey pants. During games, the black was coming off onto the pants and we looked so dirty! We didn't care, though, this was a first for everyone involved, and we were thrilled to be a part of it. The fans were so into it, watching women's hockey at that level and cheering on the different countries. That was the big kickoff to women's hockey in Canada, and we had some large crowds that came out to watch us play. This was also the first time that the best women's players from all over Canada were put on the same team. We had doctors and trainers that took care of whatever we needed. If someone blocked a shot or they had a cut, the team doctor was there to sew it up right away. I have so many fond memories of that tournament.

It was a successful tournament all around, with good teams from other nations and slow but promising growth in popularity. Over the next several years, I played in the tournament, representing my country, three more times. In every case, the gold medal came down to a game against the U.S., which we always managed to win. I have to hand it to the U.S. team, which got better every time we faced them.

I was at the top of my game and feeling good about hockey. And life was pretty good all around. I'd graduated from Seneca College with a diploma in Recreation Facilities Management and was hired by the school as a sports programmer in 1985. But my sights were set on the coming 1998 Olympic Games in Nagano, Japan, which would feature the first women's Olympic hockey tournament. The game had been steadily growing, and this felt like a huge recognition.

But I was passed over. The women's game is a pretty small world. Many of us knew each other from various girls and women's teams or were at least familiar with each other from provincial championships in the past. And I'd had successes at the highest levels, playing with excellent teams. So it hurt to not be selected for Team Canada in Nagano. I saw great players get picked to represent Canada, women I'd competed with and played against. I really felt I belonged.

As many expected, Team Canada faced the U.S. for the gold medal. And like every other Canadian, all I could do was watch on TV as the game tilted towards an American victory. I can't say if my being there would have made a difference, but it was so hard to watch, not able to even try to help turn things around.

Playing hockey was really tough after that. I was invited to the Three Nations Cup, and I had my six-week-old son with me. The Three Nations Cup was an elite international hockey event with Canada, the USA, and Finland competing against each other. I thought we had damaged my son's eardrums, but he slept through all of the cheering. I went because I wanted to see if I could still compete at a high level. And I wanted to know if the people who cut me from the Olympic roster were wrong, or if I was wrong. It was a great event but, in a way, I was just going through the motions. My heart wasn't in it. The tournament did end well for us, with a shootout victory over the U.S. to win the Cup. But after that, I didn't play much longer before I called it quits.

By that time, all of my focus was on my day job as the sports coordinator at the Seneca College King Campus. Working with the kids was a lot of fun. I didn't flaunt anything about my hockey career, I just came to work every day and did my thing (there were some kids that knew about my career). I used to advise athletic leaders at the school, and in that I became a sort of counselor to students. They would google me and find out about me and my career. Then it would hit them, and they would freak out a little bit. Some of the students would come by my office and want pictures and autographs.

To this day, even after retiring from my position at Seneca, I still get notes from former students. I've received some beautiful letters telling me how much they appreciated me paying it forward. I loved the fact that I was able to be with students and through sports, help change their lives.

When asked, I would share my story and try to help any way I could. When it comes to certain parts of my life, especially my personal life, I really don't like to talk about myself. But sometimes I have to put myself in uncomfortable situations in order to help the cause of women's hockey. If I don't, if I'm not willing to, then I can't really say anything about why things aren't improving in women's hockey. It is important to me that I help different associations and causes, and I try to whenever they ask. I have tough time saying no (I have student managers who work with me who can say no for me, which helps).

I'd been involved with refereeing and coaching at various levels in the eighties and nineties and continued with that, too. Hockey has always been my life and I've enjoyed working with people at the grassroots level, and all the way up to national teams. There were great women before me who paved the way for us to play on the biggest national stages and it's our duty to do what we can to keep the game growing.

After I retired from hockey, there was some talk about me being inducted into the Hockey Hall of Fame. I didn't think much about it until 2008, when I was inducted into the International Ice Hockey Federation Hall of Fame. I was recognized for my 50 games in total for Team Canada, as well as scoring contributions and my role in the game, generally. It was a tremendous honour.

When I first got the call, I was incredulous. René Fasel of the IIHF called while I was at work. I thought it was my buddy, Steve, playing a prank. I told him, "Quit fooling around! Steve, I know it's you."

René said, "No, it is true, this is Mr. Fasel."

It took a few exchanges like that before it finally sunk in and I realized it was really him!

Cammi Granato, Geraldine Heaney, and I were inducted together. We were the first group of women to go into the Hall. It was an eye-opener for hockey all over the world, and other organizations began to recognize women, too. As well they should, because the world was changing for the better.

The 2008 event took place in Quebec City. My family came with me, and it was such a wonderful ceremony. My kids were really young at the time. The IIHF had put us up in a posh hotel, and my mom and my other family were staying at a nearby Super 8. My mom had been sitting down for a while, then she got up to go walk, and when she was on the sidewalk, her legs gave out and she fell. My poor mom, her face was all scraped up and she was a mess. They walked into the reception and my mom looked like she got beat up. My little kids got ahold of some crayons and started writing on the walls of our room in this posh hotel. I ended up giving my mom and my family the nice hotel, and I took the kids and went to the Super 8.

Following the IIHF event in Quebec City, that is when I started to think that one day, a woman would be inducted into the Hockey Hall of Fame.

The day I got the call that I was going to be inducted into the Hall of Fame, I had taken a day off work and decided to go out for a drink with my partner. We went over to a pub, and while sitting there a story came on the TV talking about the Hockey Hall of Fame and who the potential next inductees might be. Ange turned to me and said, "Hey, what do you think?" I just sort of blew it off. It didn't seem likely at the time. We finished our drink and went home.

I was upstairs when the phone rang. "This is Jim Gregory, and I am sitting around the table with Pat Quinn and a number of the other officials, and we don't want you to say anything to anybody. But we want to tell you that you are going to be inducted into the Hockey Hall of Fame." The day was Tuesday, June 22, 2010, a day that I will never forget.

I was stunned, but I didn't want to make the same mistake as when the IIHF called me. They were on the intercom system, and I heard, "Hi Angela, this is Pat Quinn here." Everyone else said hi, and I can't remember all of their names because I was overwhelmed. At the end they reminded me to not tell anybody. But when I got off the phone, I called my mom right away.

And then the world got turned upside down. Everyone wanted to speak to me. I don't know how people got my address, but they would knock on my door. I had a ten-year-old and four-year-old twins, and the house was going crazy. The whole thing was a whirlwind.

Ange said, "Do you understand what is happening?"

I looked at her and said, "Not really!"

The night of the induction in November 2010 was surreal. As one of the first women inducted, I felt I was representing female players from around the world. In my speech, I talked about how hockey had been my savior. It made me all the more determined to make the women's game bigger and better.

I was so scared standing up in front of everyone. I was so nervous when I started to speak. I was glad the lights were shining on my eyes, because that way I couldn't see too many people. I didn't know what I should say or what I shouldn't say. I know I wrote my speech, and then afterwards people asked me, "Who wrote your speech?" I had to admit that I wrote it. I didn't really understand the significance of what happened that night for quite some time after the fact. I know while it was happening, it was a crazy night with the media and everything like that. The last time I had anywhere close to that much attention was when I wasn't selected for the Olympic team in 1998. But the night of the induction, I was still a little guarded with the media. As they spoke to me, I kind of thought to myself, *Is this real? Do I deserve this?* But the greatest thing about a member of the Hockey Hall of Fame is the way my family and partner are treated. We are pretty good judges of people, and everyone at the Hall is genuine and the people who work there don't discriminate. The staff at the Hall do a great job of living out the dreams of the ones that are being inducted. I felt so welcomed and I felt like I was part of a special fraternity. The other members of the Hall that were around that night were terrific. They all genuinely wanted to get to know me and talk to me. The more I talked to the other members of the Hall, the more I realized that we had a lot of similar stories when it came to the love of hockey and what it took to be inducted.

Being inducted the same night as someone like Cammi Granato was important to me. I was Canadian, and Cammi is American. It was important for hockey and important for the Hall of Fame to get it right, and they did. I certainly didn't want to be the only woman being inducted that night. Plus, Cammi's pedigree is phenomenal. She had a great career, and she has brothers who played and coached. Her family was from Chicago, and my family was from Toronto, both Original Six cities.

Along with some other great hockey players who weren't inducted that night, I feel we paved the way for what is happening now in women's hockey. A new generation of players is growing our great game, and I hope they do the same, blazing a broader path for the next generation.

The next goal is to develop a successful professional women's league. There have been attempts, but for different reasons none have found firm footing yet. Perhaps it starts with growing the game at the university and college level. And we need to get other countries from around the world to help grow the game as well.

People always ask me about women in hockey and, to be honest, hockey is behind other sports. If you look at basketball and football, they are so far ahead of hockey when it comes to women involved at the pro level. If hockey is for everyone like they say, then it has to be for men *and* women.

I know they are working to groom more women to be officials. They also need a training centre to develop more women coaches and the same goes for hockey administration. I always look to the NBA and basketball as an example. The NBA has had women officials for the longest time. They have women who work in the front office, and now we are seeing women coaching at the top levels. It all comes down to respecting women and treating them like professionals.

Throughout my career, and even afterwards, it has been a struggle for women's hockey to get the recognition we deserve. Women, no matter what, always take a backseat. Even today, in golf and tennis and soccer, women don't get the same support as men. I am talking about better access to training facilities, better travel, better accommodations, better media support, and better corporate sponsorships. And it's not just Canada. In Russia, women's hockey receives very little respect. Back in my heyday, the *North York Mirror* would do the occasional write-up, but other than that, women's hockey didn't get a lot of media attention. CBC covered the national championship in Quebec one year, but that was about it.

Hockey is slowly getting better, and the old bias and prejudice in the game is gradually dying off. And the game of hockey has evolved; it is more a skill game now. Everything has to evolve, and the next step is, hopefully, more women participating in all aspects of the game.

When I am not with my family or when I was helping to coach the

Toronto Six of the old Premier Hockey Federation, I love watching our current national team. These women are so good, and the level of skill within the country has greatly improved. These star players had a tough time even making Team Canada for the 2022 Olympics; the competition was that stiff leading up to the games. I am proud to see players like Natalie Spooner do so well. I love watching Sarah Nurse and Marie-Philip Poulin, Captain Clutch. The coaches did an excellent job keeping them all engaged and in the program throughout Covid, working them to be better athletes. It was impressive.

That dedication is why Team Canada won by such a lopsided score in the preliminary rounds during the 2022 Olympics. With the exception of a close gold medal win over the USA, Canada hammered Sweden and Switzerland in the quarterfinals and the semifinals. My hope is that the program can sustain that level of training so that Team Canada is always number one.

I want to ensure my children have a different experience of the game than I did, and an easier start to life, too. I am proud of my hockey accomplishments, but I am prouder of my children.

My oldest son is a lot like me, humble and quiet. He played some junior hockey in Hearst, Ontario, in the NOJHL (Northern Ontario Junior Hockey League) and I went to some games. When they hosted a big tournament, I went and did a little talk, but I try not to get in the way.

My other son is much the same when it comes to being modest. He told me a story about what happened in high school one day. He said, "I walked into the classroom and these two boys were having a conversation about the Toronto Six hockey team."

I said, "Oh, Michael, did you say that your mom helps coach the team?"

He said, "No!"

All I could do was laugh. I try to allow my kids to live their lives. My daughter is the one who brags about me the most. When she was seven years old, one of the other kids said something to her that bugged her, so she looked at this kid and said, "Do you know who my mother is?"

We still laugh at that story.

My kids liked the video tribute TSN did for me in 2021, featuring a great rap song from Keysha Freshh, for my induction into the Order of Hockey. I loved it. I thought it was very moving. It was great to see how Keysha saw me and where I came from. It was a great look back at my journey from Flemingdon Park to the Hockey Hall of Fame.

Not long ago, they renamed the Flemingdon Park arena: it's now the Angela James Arena. Of all the honours I've received, perhaps that one says the most.

2

Condition Your Mind

Mark Borowiecki

Some people are electricians, or journalists, or engineers. I am just a guy who plays hockey. I'm not special or any better than anyone else. I just have a different skill set than some people, and I've tried to do the best I can with it.

I have been pretty fortunate in my life and in my career playing in the NHL, and I think you have to pay it forward. Giving back and getting involved with charity work is the right thing to do.

———

My wife, Tara, and I have the same values, and we want to raise our children to be inclusive and accepting. Those values go back to my time growing up in Ottawa, in a house that backs onto a hydro line easement. It wasn't technically our backyard, but there was this big, flat space that felt like ours. My dad would always build an outdoor rink there. Because of that, I started skating when I was really young, learning with my dad and my older sister. Right away, I fell in love with skating and being on the ice.

I started playing organized hockey when I was five years old, and early on in my minor hockey career I started playing rep hockey. I progressed quickly, which is fairly typical for most guys who go on to play in the NHL.

It wasn't all a straight line, though. At one point, I took some time off from AA hockey, dropping down a level to A hockey. I wasn't sure what I was going to do in the future, and at the time I just wanted to have fun playing hockey with my friends. But soon I decided I wanted the greater competition and went back to playing AA and then AAA hockey.

After playing Minor Midget, I wasn't drafted into Major Junior hockey. I wasn't even drafted into Tier 2 Junior hockey. I ended up going back and playing a Major Midget year, which is uncommon for guys who go on to competitive careers.

If hockey wasn't going to work out, I was more than ready to pursue my education. I was preparing to apply to RMC, the Royal Military College, in Kingston, Ontario. I also considered going to school and playing hockey at Carleton University or the University of Ottawa.

But then at the end of my Major Midget year we won the City of Ottawa championship. Out of that, I was drafted by the Smiths Falls Bears of the Tier 2 Canadian Junior Hockey League (CJHL). At that point, I felt I had an opportunity to do something. I had a good rookie season my first year in Smiths Falls. The Barrie Colts were checking me out, and so was Drummondville of the QMJHL (Quebec Maritimes Junior Hockey League). However, my parents were set on the NCAA route as the best for me. Considering how things in hockey had gone for me, they had a point. I was playing well, but a strong pro career wasn't guaranteed, and I needed to think about my future.

In the 2007–2008 season with Smiths Falls, I had committed to playing hockey and going to school at Clarkson University in Potsdam, New York. Our coach in Smiths Falls, Bill Bowker, is one of my hockey mentors. Bill had a lot of influence on me and was always very open and supportive. He didn't get into any specifics, but he did tell me there were a few teams sniffing around and asking questions about me. He never said anything about the NHL, but I knew there was some interest in me.

And then I was drafted by the Ottawa Senators in the fifth round of the 2008 NHL entry draft. It was a surprise. The Dallas Stars and the Florida Panthers had talked to me, but I never had an interview with anyone from the Senators. But the plan for now was the same. After I got drafted, I went off to Clarkson for my first year at university. I have always enjoyed school and was a decent student. I was a political science major at Clarkson. It's more of a business and engineering school, but I love reading and writing. To this day, I read a ton.

Our coach at Clarkson was George Roll. I loved playing for him. The whole coaching staff showed a lot of belief and trust in me. They played me in a lot of different roles, and I got exposed to different situations on the ice. They relied on me heavily right from my freshman year. I didn't come into the program as an offensive guy—I was more a shut-down defenceman at the beginning. But as I got more comfortable, they used me in more offensive roles. As I enjoyed success offensively, it rounded out my game. I am still in touch with George.

He treated me as a human first and a hockey player second. That left a good impression on me.

At Clarkson, there was as big emphasis on the gym. At the time, I whined and moaned about it. Looking back, all that time in the gym helped me physically and mentally. It didn't just strengthen me, it also made me realize the benefits of my physical attributes. I got a lot stronger in the gym, and I got a lot stronger on the ice. I centred my game on my strength. All that emphasis on training at Clarkson really helped.

Back in my second year with the Smiths Falls Bears, I had only weighed 159 pounds and I was just over six feet tall. I was getting destroyed on the ice. When I left Clarkson after three years, I was close to two hundred pounds. Our training at Clarkson was intense, and not just in-season. We didn't have a ton of success on the ice, so that led to some nasty workouts for the entire team in the spring. That taught me some good lessons and the importance of a good work ethic. Hard work and my first real taste of independence were two of the biggest lessons I learned at Clarkson. Commitment to workouts, training, taking care of myself, and living away from my parents. We worked hard there in the gym and on the ice. I had a great group of teammates who enjoyed suffering physically a bit together. It brought us all closer and turned us into men.

I don't think I would have played pro hockey without the on- and off-ice lessons in work ethic I learned at Clarkson. Like I mentioned previously, we worked hard, and I was fortunate to have a group of classmates and best friends who all embraced that hard work. Our teams weren't the most successful on-ice, but in hindsight, those tough spring workouts as a sort of punishment for a poor season were formative for me as a man and as an eventual pro hockey player. I still look back on those early mornings of really hard physical work with gratitude to my coaches and peers. They sucked at the time, I won't lie. But they made me who I am.

After I left Clarkson, I had a cup of coffee, a short stint, in Binghamton with the AHL Senators. I now had the strength of a man, and I was able to impose myself physically in the AHL right from the get-go. But they decided they didn't need me, so they sent me back to school.

Then they had a rash of injuries and they needed bodies. They called me back to Bingo, and I ended up playing almost all of the playoffs. (For those who don't speak hockey, Bingo is player slang for Binghamton.) We went on to beat the Houston Aeros in the Final and won the Calder Cup as champions of the American Hockey League. I was put in a good role as a second- or third-pair defenceman and played a lot on the penalty kill. It was all an awesome experience as a young player.

For the next few years, I bounced back and forth between the Binghamton Senators and the Ottawa Senators. During one of my call-ups, in November 2013, I scored my first NHL goal, and against Carey Price! In the basement of my home, I have a big picture of me celebrating that goal with Marc Methot, Kyle Turris, and Clarke MacArthur. That was a special moment, for sure. That night, after the game, I went back to my room at the Holiday Inn in Kanata, just outside of Ottawa, and I couldn't sleep. I was too excited after scoring my first NHL goal.

From there, I feel like everything fell into place nicely in my life. I married Tara in 2014. By the start of the 2014–2015 season, I was a full-time member of the Ottawa Senators and never went back to the AHL. To fans, it looked like I had the perfect life. However, something was wrong, and I didn't even know it. It took Tara to point out to me what wasn't right.

I always was the kind of person who liked to train on my own. I would work with the strength coaches in Ottawa, listening to what they told me, but then do the work on my own at home. I always liked getting away from the rink and having a different environment. I found it less intimidating and I was less anxious working out at home. I never had an issue being motivated to train. To this day, working out in the gym is an outlet for my negative energy.

But I was having these insane adrenaline rushes at two or three in the morning, and I was filled with this dark, negative energy. The only way for me to get that out was physical exertion. Even though it was so late at night, I would go into my home gym and crush myself with an intense workout. I would then be exhausted the rest of the day from the combination of working out and the adrenaline dump from the panic attack. Because that's what they were: panic attacks.

It took a toll on my relationship with Tara. I was becoming distant and closed off. I was scared to admit that something might be wrong with me and that I needed help. She finally said to me, "I think you need help. I need you to get help for our sake." Thankfully, she pushed me in the right direction.

I had to miss a trip to Sweden with the Senators in November 2017 to deal with my mental health. Well, Sweden wasn't going anywhere, and my mental health was a bigger priority. And Tara was right, I did need help.

As my NHL career progressed, I had gotten away from the idea of having fun and loving the game. I had put a lot of pressure on myself to have success, provide for my family, and hold up my end of the bargain as a player. But all of that had a negative effect on my game on the ice, and my life off the ice.

There were times that my thoughts made me feel guilty. After all, I had a great life, was well paid. I didn't really want for anything and my kids were going to be set. I had to wonder, why was I feeling these emotions?

The stress and pressure is part of the job—hockey is a results-driven industry. When those results don't come to you easily or naturally, they can lead you down some dark roads.

I had been signed as a free agent by Nashville. I was diagnosed with obsessive-compulsive disorder in my first year there. I always knew there was something gnawing at me in the back of my mind. I think OCD has been a blessing and a curse for me as pro. My obsessive tendencies led to a deep commitment to training, nutrition, and routines. But it was so hard to find a balance and make those commitments sustainable in the long run. I tended to grind myself down and burn myself out.

Using a lot of the resources available to me and our team psychiatrist in Nashville helped me as I entered the 2021–2022 season.

I was able to re-centre myself. I realized that success comes from having fun and enjoying the game. You are not going to play to your potential or have the kind of success you are capable of if you are in a bad place mentally.

I underestimated how stressful that change would be. I was a comfort player. I liked having a familiar staff, familiar surroundings, familiar faces. The change definitely threw me off more than I thought. I really wanted to show what I can do and be everything to everyone in a positive way. I think I forgot to just focus on myself as a player and on my family. It took a big toll on me.

In fall 2021, I spoke to *The Athletic* about my struggles with mental health and how I had been trying to deal with it. Anytime I have talked openly about it, a bunch of players from around the NHL have reached out to me. That's always been appreciated, but I want to be clear that I wasn't looking for support.

When I first came into the NHL, I was so scared to talk about mental health because I thought it was going to make me look weak or negatively affect my career. I want this next generation of players and the next generation of athletes in all sports to realize that you are not the only one having these emotions. I want them to look at me. I have played over a decade in pro hockey with this, and I managed to deal with it. I had to learn there was a better way for me to deal with it, but when I was young, I was scared to get a handle on it. Hopefully, when the time is right, other athletes will know it is important for them to get the help that they need.

I don't have any professional training when it comes to mental health, I'm no expert. But anecdotally, for what I have been through at this stage in my career, I can see things I never noticed before. There are times I can see young guys who are struggling. And it isn't just young guys. It is scary for NHL players who want to get help. There is still a negative connotation that you are showing weakness or teams will second-guess your value if you seek help. The more of us that talk about it, the more guys will realize that it is normal. Because I got help, I enjoy hockey now. Prior to that, I definitely went through some periods where hockey was a grind for me. Deep down, I still loved it. But there was so much white noise in my head.

I am now in a really good place. My job is being a hockey player, but it is not my entire identity. At this point in my life, I am first and foremost a good husband and a good father. That is what drives me in this competitive environment. Being in the best shape physically is what motivates me and keeps me happy. But because I got professional help, I have better skills and tactics to deal with mental health problems when they arise.

A sports psychologist I worked with likened working on your mental health to working out in the gym. I hated hitting the gym all the time in university, but it was part of the job. Taking care of your mental health is no different. The idea is that you do physical reps all summer to get strong—well, how much have you focused on your mental reps? The more that you do those mental reps, the more they will become ingrained in you.

I have worked on skills that will help me in situations where I need to be resilient. I am not going to say that I will be able to handle things perfectly, but I know I am able to handle things a lot better than before. A, because when I feel that way again, I know what it is, and I am not going to die from it or get hurt. And B, I practiced being prepared for these situations.

I don't wake up at two in the morning and work out anymore, but sleep is still an issue. A lot of athletes have a hard time sleeping. I don't have a hard time falling asleep. My issue is staying asleep until the morning. I am always up and ready to go and do something. I think a lot of it is that anxious energy that I have. I consider sleeping in past 6:30 in the morning a win. In the NHL, the schedule dictates when you go to bed and when you can sleep a little more. Still, my goal as the season goes on is to be able to sleep a little more every night.

I am not going to lie and say that I have fixed all of my problems. These are things I am going to have to deal with the rest of my life. I don't think sleeping as little as I do is sustainable or the healthiest thing, but for whatever reason, this is the way I am wired, and I know I'm not the only one. When I was in a negative place, I was ready to get up and do something aggressive or physical. I still wake up early, but now it is more a case of how to set the structure of my day properly and make sure that I am healthy and ready to go. To help with my mental health, I journal. It gives me peace of mind and helps centre me. And that is something I carry over from the off-season and into the season. I like writing, and journaling is a good outlet for me, so I've made it part of my daily routine. I don't like to write negative stuff. I spend a lot of time writing to my young son, Myles. This is stuff he can read down the road to learn about me. Hopefully, it will give him strength if he ever has to deal with any similar issues.

The world is changing and the pressure on young people is changing daily. There's constant pressure to always be in the limelight, and social media is everywhere. The world is much more fast-paced than it was, and unfortunately with that change comes some negative things, too.

I used to get really hung up on what people said on social media and the internet when I was younger. It was tough. For a time, I shied away from social media because I was scared of the negative aspect of it. Now, I take social media for what it is. I realized that my Instagram is mine, and I can control it. I view it as a way to give people insight to who I am as a person, not just the guy on the ice. Me, in a hockey jersey, that is just a part of my identity. My value and worth as a human being isn't tied to my success on the ice.

Hopefully, some other young athletes can see that from my Instagram and learn from it. The more you have your personal life in order, and are happy about it, the better you are going to perform in your sport.

My first year in Nashville, I had a vision I was going to do all these things. I wanted to be everything to everyone in Nashville. I wanted to be a leader on the team, I wanted to be a solid defenceman, I wanted to chip in offensively, I wanted to connect with the coaches, with management, and with the fans. I wanted to be involved in the community and it all just overwhelmed me.

Now, I am able to reset and look at it better. I realized that my goals coming into Nashville were still reachable, especially now that I was in a better place. I was better able to handle the bumps that were going to come along the way, and I was really excited for the future in Nashville. I enjoyed every minute of my NHL career, and retired on May 3, 2023, after playing 458 games over 12 seasons.

I have had some old friends in the hockey industry who are involved in youth teams or college teams reach out to me and say, "Hey, I have read your story to my players." My response is always, "If you have guys or girls who need an athlete to talk to, give them my number." I don't just want young athletes to read about my story, I want them to use me as a resource. I am in the game, I understand the daily ups and downs of an athlete, and hopefully I can be a help to others.

I have climbed some of these mountains and handled these issues. Sometimes I did it the right way, and sometimes I did the wrong way. I may never get it perfect, and that's okay. Through it all, I learn.

After a ten-year hiatus from my school days, I am proud to say that I am back finishing up my final year of credits online. I was able to take my three years of credits at Clarkson University and transfer them to a history degree at Arizona State. History has always been a passion. Eventually, I would like to get my master's degree in medieval history.

Never stop learning. Never stop growing. You just never know what the future holds.

3

Hockey Card Collector

Dean Barnes

I have a unique hockey card collection, and like any collector, I enjoy showing it to people. But with my collection, there's always an "aha" moment when someone sees how many Black players made it to the NHL.

I have an NHL Black hockey card collection of one hundred cards of Black and biracial players who have played at least one NHL game. I started collecting cards when I was seven years old and recently started my collection again during the pandemic. My collection was featured in the NHL Black Hockey History Mobile Museum and has been very influential for enabling Black and biracial children and parents to see themselves in the game in Canada and the United States. I have also established relationships with former players who are grateful that their stories are becoming better known by people throughout the world. I have even interviewed Willie O'Ree, the first Black to play in the NHL, and many others.

I also have a successful podcast called *My Hockey Hero*, which is sponsored by eBay Canada. I have interviewed Black and biracial players from my card collection in this podcast, through which I made it possible for a corporate donation to be made to Hockey Equality, a hockey organization that reduces financial barriers for Black, Indigenous, female, and other equity-deserving groups to access the game. My podcast won Best Sports Podcast at the Black Podcasting Awards in August 2023. My current podcast is balanced in its delivery and is designed to share the stories of the players in an inspirational way. I have now interviewed twenty-seven former players from my card collection, and the podcast has ranked as high as fifteenth overall in the United States and in the top twenty-five Canadian Apple podcast rankings at times.

The collection is a bit of a teaching tool when it comes to racialized minorities. And I think it's important to give these players credit and help tell their stories. It is so hard to make it to the NHL, to achieve that goal, no matter what colour the player. I should know. Long before I started collecting hockey cards, particularly *these* cards, I was a kid growing up in Burlington, Ontario. My parents are Jamaican and immigrated to Canada, via England. I have an older brother and sister who were born in England, but I was born in Hamilton, before we moved to Burlington, where I started kindergarten. It wasn't long before I started playing hockey, when I was around six years old.

In the beginning, I played at an outdoor rink in Burlington run by the Kiwanis Club, and it had cage fencing around the boards. I learned to skate there and I went to public skating with my sister, Karen. I always played road hockey, too, with my brother and his friends behind the local elementary school. Maybe playing with older kids helped me develop faster. I started playing house league hockey, and then I made the jump to AA in Minor Atom. From the time I was ten years old, I was playing AAA, and never went back. As a young kid there wasn't a lot of diversity in hockey, and the demographics of the Burlington region reflected that. But I did participate in hockey with friends who had parents who were new to the country.

High school hockey was really big at the time. If you didn't make the Junior B Burlington Cougars, you played high school hockey. I tried to make the Cougars when I was seventeen years old. I played high school hockey for two years and then played Junior B in Kitchener with the Kitchener Dutchmen at nineteen. High school hockey was very competitive and filled with former rep players because you had to choose to play high school and could not play rep at the same time.

Our high school team, at Aldershot High, won the local high school hockey championship, and we just missed going to the OFSAA (Ontario Federation of School Athletic Association) Provincial High School Championships (for the best teams in Ontario).

When I graduated high school, I was recruited to try out at the University of Waterloo. I didn't make it my first year—many freshmen don't—so I played Junior B for the Kitchener Dutchmen. By my second year, I was playing varsity for the Waterloo Warriors hockey team. Geoff Ward, who had been the coach of the Calgary Flames, was an assistant coach with the Warriors the year I played. Both Geoff Ward and Don McKee, the head coach, were very good teachers of the game and led our team to a top ten ranking in the Canadian Intercollegiate Athletic Union (CIAU) at the time.

By my third year, I had a co-op job at the University of Guelph. I was offered a job but decided to work at the University of Guelph in the recreation department, as an intramural coordinator. At that time, I was going in a different direction, more focused on my academics. My major was sport management with a minor in political science.

At one time, I was offered a job with the Hamilton Redbirds minor league baseball team from the New York–Penn league. But I didn't take it. After I graduated from Waterloo, I took a co-op job teaching at the Peel Board of Education. Then I went to teachers college at the University of Toronto, deferring my acceptance to do a master's at Queen's University. I wanted to begin teaching after a year of studies. This allowed me to teach and complete my master's part-time.

I was teaching at the North York Board of Education at the same time, which had a different feel from what I grew up with. The schools I was working in had a large number of students who were visible minorities. I started a girls hockey program at Woodbine Junior High in North York, where I was a physical education teacher.

I worked my way up and became a department head for phys-ed with the North York Board of Education. From there, I was shortlisted to become a vice principal. I was a teacher for eight years at both junior high and high school.

I had been commuting for all those years from my home in Burlington. That was a *long* commute every day. I had an opportunity to take a job closer to home in Milton, so that is what I did. In 2000, I was back in my hometown school board, working as a vice principal. I have been in school administration since then.

Around 2014, I completed my PhD at the University of Toronto. I studied for my doctorate part-time, while I was working as principal at T.A. Blakelock High School in Oakville. It was a heavy workload, but it was also a very fulfilling challenge. I was passionate about education and opportunities in education, and I was thrilled when I was finished.

I love education, and my career, but I never gave up my passion for hockey. The George Floyd protests brought a lot to the surface for a lot of people, but even before that, there were issues in hockey about inclusion.

When I think about the few Black players in the NHL then, that was fairly proportionate to the number of people who were of colour in the Burlington area when I was young. I would see kids here and there who were like me, but not many. I know that when I was at Waterloo, I was probably one of the only Black players in hockey at that level at the time.

If you look at my card collection, there are parallels there. As Canada became more diverse, you could see more Black players making it to the NHL. All of a sudden, the NHL had players such as Jarome Iginla, Mike Grier, Jamal Mayers, Anson Carter, and many others. I wanted to pay tribute to all the Black players who made it to pro hockey, no matter how short a career they had. There were a number of good Black hockey players in Canada and the United States who were just a step away from making it.

One of the cards I have is of Darren Lowe, who played eight games with the Pittsburgh Penguins. When I was at Waterloo, Darren was an assistant coach at the University of Toronto. He ended up coaching at U of T for twenty years. I read an article that he scored one goal in the NHL during his eight games with the Penguins. I thought it was a cool story, and he'd always have the bragging rights of making it that far: playing in the NHL. And to top it off, he scored a goal.

When I was young, I saw hockey cards for Mike Marson and Bill Riley (teammates on the Washington Capitals). I didn't think it was too big a deal at the time. I was the only Black kid I could see playing AAA, so it made sense to me that there were only a handful of Black players in the NHL.

Another card I love is my Mike McHugh. Following Val James, McHugh was the second African American player to make the NHL. The rest of the Black players in the NHL were Canadian.

I collect cards and some other keepsakes for different reasons. I still have a Wayne Gretzky rookie card, and I played against Wayne's younger brother Glen when I was growing up. Glen played in our age group for the Brantford AAA team. I played against their brother Brent, too, when I played for the Kitchener Dutchmen. And I have a program at home from a tournament I played in for the Burlington AAA when we faced Brendan Shanahan's team when I was twelve.

But I'm mostly on the hunt for cards of Black players. I have a Dale Craigwell card. Before he played for the San Jose Sharks, he was a teammate of Eric Lindros with the Oshawa Generals. eBay has been pretty good as a resource. I found a guy named Alton White who played in the WHA. He played for the Los Angeles Sharks. He broke into the WHA just before Mike Marson started playing for the Washington Capitals in the NHL. Alton probably could have made the NHL but decided on the Sharks (who probably paid better).

I brought the late Herb Carnegie to one of my schools in the early 2000s to speak to the students.

I had heard about his accomplishments through the Future Aces educational program, which was available to schools.

The students and staff were very inspired by Mr. Carnegie, and we effectively implemented his Character Education program in our school.

Everyone knows about Tony McKegney, who was one of the first Black stars. He was the second overall pick in the Ontario Hockey Association Major Junior draft in 1974 by the Kingston Canadians. He won a bronze medal for the Canada World Junior team in 1978 and was drafted number thirty-two overall by the Buffalo Sabres in 1978. He had eight 20-goal seasons and played in the NHL from 1978 to 1990. He ended his career with 320 goals and he was the first Black player to score 40 goals in a season. He was an inspirational player to many Black and racialized people, as it gave them someone to look up to who had made it to the NHL and achieved tremendous success.

Tony's s brother Mike played in the OHL for the Kitchener Rangers. He was a really good player in junior, but he didn't make it to the pros, and that is why he doesn't have a card.

I was lucky enough to meet Tony McKegney when I was young and playing AAA hockey. I helped run a hockey camp that Tony was a part of and as a result, a few of us got free tickets to see the Sabres play a game in Buffalo. The Sabres were hoping to draw people from the Hamilton and Burlington area and get them to buy tickets for their games. Tony had some good years in the NHL.

There certainly weren't many Black players, but it turns out there were more than I knew. When I was young, I honestly didn't know that Dirk Graham of the Blackhawks has Black ancestors. When I started doing research for my collection, I found out about Dirk's background. He was the first Black captain in the NHL.

Brian Johnson was the first Black player to play for the Red Wings, and I am still trying to find his card. He played for a short stint during Steve Yzerman's rookie year, in the 1983–1984 season.

And there are Black players who played in the AHL but never made it to the NHL. I'm still trying to find cards for many of them, guys like Darren Lowe and Steven Fletcher. Sometimes the teams would make "fake" cards for their players, guys like Val James. Born in Florida, Val James moved to New York State at a young age. He learned to skate at the rink his dad worked at as the manager. Drafted by the Red Wings in the sixteenth round of the 1977 draft, Val played seven games in the NHL, including four with the Maple Leafs in the 1986–1987 season.

If you only played in the AHL, they were not official cards. I had custom cards made for a few players. Val James had only played a small number of games in the NHL. I was able to include him in my set that was loaned to the NHL museum. This was the NHL's Black Hockey History Mobile Museum. It was part of the league's diversity initiative during the 2021–2022 season.

When I played high school hockey, we would always look forward to David Grossman's rankings in the *Toronto Star* to see if we made the top ten, which was a big deal. So when an article was published in the paper about my card collection, it was really exciting. I have been able to connect with a number of people. Some tell me that they think it's a great project, which always feels good, but I'm always eager to hear from anyone who can help me track down an elusive card.

One card I'd love to get is Bernie Saunders, the fifth black player in the NHL. His brother was the late longtime ESPN sportscaster John Saunders. I had a good phone conversation with Bernie, and he was really appreciative that I was bringing the history of Black players in the NHL to light. I wasn't able to speak with the Maple Leafs' John Craighead but Bernie reached out to me when he read my story on NHL.com. Bernie wanted to pass on his support for what I was doing, and I later was able to interview Bernie on the *My Hockey Hero* podcast.

Another player I am interested in is former Vancouver Canucks forward Nathan LaFayette. Nathan is biracial, and I had a good exchange with him on LinkedIn. He is a nice guy, and I actually played pickup hockey with him when I was working at another school in Oakville.

These guys who once played in the NHL all went on to have successful business careers. For some of them, it's been fifteen or twenty years since they played.

I enjoy collecting the cards, hunting them down, and when I'm very fortunate, getting to speak to the players themselves. But I want to find a way to share my collection with hockey fans around North America and around the world. That's my next step.

I have some connections with the NHL's diversity program (though I've yet to hear from the NHL itself). I am trying to get my card collection on the mobile Black History Month celebration. We want the game to grow, and we don't want any barriers to participation. Maybe by sharing this card collection, everyone can learn from history.

There are probably other Black people like me who grew up with the same experience. For me it's a kind of giving back, trying to contribute to the telling of these untold stories of success of Black players in the NHL.

I am sure a lot of people have heard of most of the names in my collection. But I don't think anyone has thought of all the Black players in their entirety in one single collection of cards. Having them together this way shows this isn't just about Black hockey history; it is a collection of hockey history. These cards all tell a story, and it's bigger than most people would ever imagine.

4

The Joy of Giving Back

Graham McWaters

have always been involved in sports. I grew up in Montreal and I played hockey and soccer as a kid. Later on, I coached hockey and soccer. At one time, I ran an adult soccer league. But as a hockey player, I never made it past Midget A hockey, only playing some intramural hockey when I went to McGill University. That's not important, though, to the work I do today.

I could make organizing the Indigenous Hockey Equipment Drive, this charity, my full-time job, if I wasn't volunteering (I still have to make a living). It just keeps getting bigger and bigger. As a young man, I never thought I would be involved in something of this magnitude, making a difference to a First Nations community. I have so many people on board with me that help me with what I am doing, the response is outrageous.

As a young man, I left Montreal just after the Canadiens won the Stanley Cup in 1986. I landed in Richmond Hill, Ontario, and I have been there ever since.

When my kids were younger, and their team needed an assistant coach or a manager, I would step in and help. Years later, my son Ryan was playing for the Richmond Hill Stars and we were at a Silver Stick tournament in Midland, Ontario. I was leaving the rink after a game, and I saw these kids walking in with plastic bags and small duffel bags holding their hockey equipment. I could see they were all Indigenous kids.

I could also see a man on his knees in the parking lot, fixing the facemask on an old helmet. It was obvious he was with the kids I had seen with the plastic bags. I walked up to him and said, "Where are you guys from?"

He said, "We are from Beausoleil First Nation, on Christian Island."

I asked him if they could use some equipment and he said, "We sure could. Let me speak to my girlfriend, Rosemarie." We exchanged phone numbers right there on the spot.

I talked to my wife, Angie, about what I wanted to do, and she was totally on board. From there, I went to Ryan's team where he was playing Midget A. I asked the coaches and the other parents what we could do. We ended up gathering up eight or nine bags of equipment and twenty-five sticks. I took all the gear and drove up to the Barrie

Native Friendship Centre to meet Rosemarie, who was based not far from there. When I arrived, there was close to thirty kids, all waiting for equipment. They had tables set up, and Rosemarie and her helpers were ready to distribute the equipment to the kids that day.

This one little boy, without any supervision, walked up and down the tables and grabbed all the equipment that he needed to play hockey. I watched as he tried on equipment without any adults assisting him. He assembled and put on the gear all by himself and he had a big smile on his face the entire time. The gear he picked up reflected how many different people and groups had contributed. A lot of people from around York Region stepped up to help us out. I could see his pants were donated by the Markham Majors AAA organization.

The next year, I went to the Richmond Hill Hockey Association directly and asked if they could help me with this. I wrote a note explaining who I was and what I was trying to do, and for whom, and they sent it out in a mass email to everyone—the teams, the parents, even sponsors. The note also said I'd be parked at the Elgin Barrow Arena in Richmond Hill from this time to this time on a certain date to receive donations. The hockey association sure didn't disappoint.

I wasn't sure how much I'd get, or what condition any of it would be in. But as people started coming over, I realized I needed a bigger truck. I was inundated with donations, gathering over thirty bags of equipment from different families. I took it all home and sorted it out: skates, helmets, and all the other gear. At first, I put it all in my basement. It filled half the space! I wasn't going to be able to keep it there for long, so the next step was to set up a date to bring it all up to Beausoleil First Nation.

It was winter, and not so easy to get to Beausoleil. I drove as far as I could and then they brought me and the equipment over to Christian Island on a ferry that broke up the ice. When I arrived, there was a ton of people waiting for us to help us sort it all. We took the ferry and then drove all of the gear to the rink where we met volunteers from the community that helped us unload everything into the rink. Once we were all done, getting everything set up by equipment type and size, they brought all of the kids in. They would grab a hockey bag and start filling it up with whatever they needed.

The first few years, Beausoleil First Nation was our only stop. Everything we collected went to people there. But the last year we went there, they gave half of the equipment to a few other First Nations communities. When I heard that, I realized we needed to do something bigger to help more people.

Not long after that, I bumped into someone I knew at the Canada Mortgage and Housing Corporation (CMHC), Terri Gibbons. Terri introduced me to someone else that worked there, Frank Horn. Frank was in charge of the Indigenous housing department. Frank knew all the Indigenous communities and had thoughts on who could use some hockey equipment. He had some other ideas, too. Frank played hockey with a guy named Randy Gill, who worked at a sports charity based in Oshawa called Their Opportunity. That organization helps pay the registration fees of various sports for kids and families who can't afford it. All they ask in return is that the family give back to the community in some way. Frank was the key to all of us connecting, and now he is one of their main volunteers.

Expanding the donations in this way meant we needed more space for storage than my basement. In 2018, I contacted the senior partner at AMJ Campbell, Denis Frappier, and talked to him about the charity. Denis was eager to help out, and AMJ donated storage space for us in Barrie, Ontario. Without that, we couldn't do this.

With so much donated equipment filling all those storage bins, we also needed better transport than my truck. We've received a lot of help from Bristol Truck Rentals. They have been very accommodating, giving me a break on the bill for the rental trucks. That has really helped us keep our costs down.

We're always looking for new donors. Through a family friend, I was able to get word to Maple Leafs Sports & Entertainment (MLSE) about what we were doing. One of the MLSE executives put me in touch with Greg Schell, who is in charge of Youth Hockey Development for the Maple Leafs. In 2019, Greg's department donated a large batch of equipment to us—brand new. The equipment was so good that every time we did a distribution of used equipment, we would include an assortment of new equipment so it got spread around. It was obvious which pieces the Leafs had given us: all the new equipment was still in their boxes.

The best thing to happen to us was when the Leafs youth program changed from CCM equipment to Bauer. It meant the Leafs had a lot of "old" CCM stuff they weren't using anymore, all this perfectly good brand-new equipment. At first, Greg told me to come with a small truck to pick up the gear, but a few weeks later he called me up and said, "Bring a bigger truck, I've got more gear for you." How much? "As much as you can take," he said. Bristol Truck Rentals was again a big help that day. The crew that runs National Training Rinks (NTR), a hockey and skating school in the area, has also been extremely helpful. They are located in Richmond Hill and owner Rick Cornacchia went out of his way to help us.

Whenever we announce that we're distributing equipment, First Nations communities come from all over. One day, a family drove five hours from Manitoulin Island. That same weekend, an elderly couple drove five hours from the Kahnawake First Nations community near Montreal. They came to Barrie in an SUV with a trailer and picked up forty bags of equipment from us.

We do several events each year, but usually around the same time. It all takes months to organize. We have to collect all the equipment, of course, then sort it, tag it, and bag it. Then we have to store it all. When the time comes, we arrange for transport and announce to communities when and where the donation is happening so they can plan for it. We have a system in place where we host around six to eight hockey drives in the first half of the year. This allows us to gather around 800 to 1,000 bags of sorted hockey gear. After that, come fall, we start distributing all the gear from Whitby, Barrie, and Sudbury, Ontario.

It's a lot to do, but nothing compared to the work on the donation day itself, and some are bigger than others. Because of Covid, we were not able to distribute equipment in 2020; that meant in fall 2021, we were busier than ever. That year we loaded 400 bags of equipment in a fifty-three-foot trailer to be shipped to Thunder Bay. At the end of a day like that, I was exhausted, but it was a good exhausted.

That Thunder Bay trip was a big one, and a lot farther away than we normally go. The bags were unloaded in Thunder Bay at a warehouse, where they stayed for three months. The group that arranged the warehouse at the airport, Indigenous Sport & Wellness Ontario, signed a three-month lease to give them a safe period of time to distribute the gear to numerous communities in and around the Thunder Bay area. They were then distributed to twenty First Nations communities in the far north of Ontario. We hired a trucking company called Bison for the twenty-hour drive from Burlington. The cost was covered by an organization called HIP, which stands for Honouring Indigenous Peoples.

We don't have to do all the heavy lifting on our own. I try to have a minimum of six volunteers for each donation day, distributing anywhere from 100 to 300 bags of equipment in a four-hour window. In

2021, members of the Burlington Cougars junior hockey team came out to help. It's great when these kids volunteer to help others like that—it's one more reason to make sure all kids can have a chance to play hockey. If we can get more kids into environments like that, we are going to help them.

This charity has grown so much. In the beginning, we were able to gather up eight bags of equipment. In 2021, we received 1,000 bags in a twelve-month period, with over 200 sets of goalie pads and over 800 sticks. I have done it so many times now, if someone contacts me that they have equipment to donate, I am ready to go. The day we load everything up to distribute, we have to have volunteers to help.

That part has been easier than I expected. Like the Thunder Bay trip, sometimes local hockey teams will help. In Newmarket, we held four events over two weekends, and there were six different hockey players at each event from the York-Simcoe Express Hockey Association. But we also have high school kids getting in the volunteer hours they need in order to graduate in Ontario. Time and energy are just as necessary as money or equipment.

It's a long day, and so it's important to keep the energy up and spirits high. I like to engage with my volunteers: talk with them, ask where they go to school, what team they play for, stuff like that. Ultimately, we talk about the charity and our most recent equipment drop-off. A number of the volunteers end up asking me if they can come back the next week, or they'll say, "Please let me know when I can do this again." I'm always thrilled to hear that. We have received many donations and need all the help we can get.

Now that the charity is more established, we receive donations from lots of different places, and they often come unexpectedly. George Burnett, the head coach and GM of the Ontario Hockey League Guelph Storm, called me up one day, introduced himself, and said, "I hear you are doing an equipment drive for First Nations communities. I used to do some stuff for Six Nations, and I have some gear for you, some practice jerseys and some sticks."

When I got to Guelph to pick it all up, I realized that some of the sticks had NHL players' names on them. These were guys who played for George and went on to the NHL, leaving behind their sticks. We included all this in that big shipment to Thunder Bay in the big trip in 2021.

I am at the point now that I receive two to three calls, text messages, or emails *a day* from people who want to donate. I drove to Thornhill, north of Toronto, to pick up two bags of equipment, and on the top of the bag, where you put your name, someone had left a note for whichever lucky kid got it: "Enjoy this stuff, and make your dreams come true!" That was nice.

I never expected the equipment drive to grow like this. Every year, it gets bigger and better. It's now at the point that I do three or four major hockey equipment drives a year. We have so much equipment now that in our storage area in Barrie, we have one locker that is all skates, one that is all helmets, and so on. We have held equipment drives in Whitby, Pickering, and Peterborough. We had too much stuff to drive it all the way back to Barrie, so we stored it in Whitby. The same thing happened after we completed an equipment drive in Kitchener-Waterloo. We got so much gear, over 300 bags in just four hours, that we had to find a place to store it all (this time in Burlington).

The person that helped me organize the event in Kitchener-Waterloo is a scout for the Owen Sound Attack, Mitchell Avis. He also does work as a consultant for Indigenous communities across Canada. Mitchell called me up out of the blue and said that he wanted to help. Mitchell consults in land use planning for First Nations communities. He also organized a one-man bike ride to raise money for our cause. Owen Sound forward Ethan Burroughs joined, too.

Mitchell had something more in mind, as well. He said, "I would like to do a bike ride from Kitchener to Owen Sound. All the money I get I will donate to you guys to buy new helmets." Two weeks later he tells me that he raised $3,800. That's a lot of new helmets. Unlike most gear, helmets actually have an expiration date (for league use, anyway), similar to car seats for babies and toddlers, so it's important to get new ones when we can.

We've had so much help from so many great people and groups. The York-Simcoe Express and the Aurora Panthers women's hockey association have both gotten involved. The Pee Wee Barrie Colts wanted to win the Chevrolet Good Deeds Cup for charity work in 2019; the entire team arrived on a team bus, all wearing matching track suits, as we were doing an equipment drive in Richmond Hill.

We were in Newmarket doing an equipment drive and a Toronto police officer in full uniform, Constable Alphonso Carter, showed up. He walked up to me and said, "I hope you don't mind, I am going to put you in touch with Anthony Stewart and his wife." The same Anthony Stewart who played over 250 games in the NHL. Then he called me over to his van and when he opened it up, stuff was falling out! Alphonso had driven around to police associations and gathered up as much gear as he could fit in the vehicle.

At another event, Joe Bowen, the longtime voice of the Maple Leafs, showed up with goalie equipment. Nobody is sure how Joe found out about us, he just showed up with gear and wanted to help.

Not everyone has equipment to give, but people have been generous with money, which is also an enormous help. Anytime we get a financial donation it goes to a special account set up by Their Opportunity. When I rent a truck, I submit an invoice to them. My only real expenses are renting trucks and paying for gas to transport the equipment, but it adds up.

Indigenous Sport & Wellness Ontario have been a big supporter for what we are doing. They help us coordinate all of the equipment going to the far north. The hockey community is a big family, and people love helping each other out. Someone in a community near Lake Erie had to close their sporting goods store, and they contacted us. They were going out of business and stepped up to help. When we showed up, they had garbage bags full of brand-new equipment that had been sitting in a barn.

So many people and so many organizations have stepped up and helped us, it is all very humbling. We have received help from the Ottawa Senators Foundation. Motorcity Mitsubishi in Oshawa donated storage space to us in Whitby for two years. A woman named Meghan Nolan-Cohen went a long way to help us find storage space in Burlington; then Mitchell Golman was kind enough to donate a large space in Burlington for one year.

I have learned that the hockey community can't wait to pitch in and help, from the biggest organizations to the individual volunteers. We all do it because it makes the people receiving the equipment outrageously happy.

I call it the Three Thank-Yous Principle. I am thanking you for donating the equipment, they are thanking me for taking the equipment, and the people getting the equipment are thanking us. When you get Three Thank-Yous in a charity, you know you are doing good work.

I am a firm believer that playing sports can make you a better person. We use sports to help kids grow to become better, healthier people. Sports help in so many ways. I was fortunate growing up. My parents could afford to put me into sports and buy me equipment. I was able to do the same for my kids. Now, I want to give back and help others.

I believe there are approximately 134 First Nations communities in Ontario. We've helped out forty-two of them as of 2021. We are putting kids into hockey who have never played or wouldn't otherwise be able to continue. And we are making sure kids have safer equipment when they do play.

In 2022, we ended up donating over 1,000 bags of equipment to various Indigenous communities across Canada, including 350 remote communities in Ontario. I picked up the equipment at the warehouse in Barrie and took it to a location in Mississauga and loaded it onto skids. From there, Gardewine Trucking put it on one of their trucks, and within thirty-six hours it was at the location.

In March 2023, we gave 42 bags of equipment and 42 sticks to former NHL great Reggie Leach. Reggie and his son did a hockey camp at an Indigenous community four hours north of Thunder Bay, Ontario.

Not long afterwards, we received another 250 bags of equipment from the Ottawa Senators Foundation.

In January of 2024, we partnered with the Greater Toronto Hockey League on an equipment drive. With the support of the GTHL, we were able to collect 150 full hockey bags of equipment, and we also collected over 200 sticks.

We have a standing offer from the Ontario Provincial Police: whenever we want, they will let us use one of their planes to ship equipment from Barrie to Thunder Bay.

Everyone is helping us and being so kind to us.

We have been up to Sudbury twice over the past two years, and each time we have delivered 150 bags of equipment. We invited five Indigenous communities and they each received 30 bags of equipment.

We also started a new fundraiser where we make orange bracelets out of orange skate laces. In the first three months of 2023, we sold $8,000 worth of bracelets.

We were up in Owen Sound at the same time Ron MacLean was there for Scotiabank Hockey Day.

In November 2023, for the first time in our nine-year history, we ventured outside of Ontario. A teacher named Vincent Mernett contacted me via email requesting assistance with hockey equipment for his school of over 300 students located in Behchoko, Northwest Territories. This community of over 1,800 Indigenous members is located just over one hour northwest of Yellowknife.

The high school is ten minutes away from the Ko Gocho Sportsplex Centre in Behchoko that houses a full-sized arena that was not being used by many youth in the community because they didn't own any hockey equipment. Our program had just distributed most of our gear to local Ontario Indigenous communities, so we completed a few drives in Richmond Hill and Sudbury to reach our goal of 100 bags.

Now that we had the equipment and lots of sticks, how do we get the gear delivered 4,500 kilometres away? We had arrangements to deliver the gear to its final destination via truck and then plane but that fell through because each group couldn't go to the other's drop-off and pickup point. To the rescue was CN—they picked up the seventeen wrapped skids from Barrie by truck and then loaded it on a train to Edmonton. Once in Edmonton the fifty-three-foot trailer was then delivered by road to Behchoko on Monday morning at 9:30 as scheduled by CN. The 100 bags of gear and 200 hockey sticks were unloaded into the rink and then taken out of their bags by student volunteers the same day.

As of December 2023, the Community Government of Behchoko has now formed a hockey association in collaboration with the Chief Jimmy Bruneau School. The youth in the community will now have an organization that will train, coach, and assist them on an ongoing basis thanks to one teacher who cared enough to reach out to our group.

Some of the Indigenous communities that benefited from the past few years of receiving equipment include: Chippewas of Nawash, Chippewas of the Thames, Garden River, Mississaugi, Thessalon Saugeen, Wahnapitae, Dokis, Henvey Inlet, Nipissing, Taykwa Tagamou, Beausoleil, Fort Albany, Wikwemikong, Shawanaga, Walpole Island, Kettle and Stony Point, Oneida Nation of the Thames, Aamjiwnaang, Moose Deer Point, Whitefish, Magnetewan, Atikameksheng, Aundeck-Omni-Kaning, M'Chigeeng, Munsee-Delaware, Chippewas of Rama, Akwesasne, Wasauksing, Pikwakanagan, Hiawatha, Chippewas of Georgina Island, and Aroland.

We were in Cochrane, Ontario, and this person met one of our volunteers. As they gathered hockey equipment for their community, the person said, "Ever since you guys have been giving us hockey equipment, we have had less youth suicides in the community."

Reggie Leach called me and thanked me numerous times for the donation of hockey equipment. Reggie said, "What you are doing is beyond just doing something good, you are saving lives."

That is why we do what we do. We know that sports and playing hockey will help them develop into healthier people, both physically and mentally.

You never know, one of them might just be the next big thing in the NHL.

https://www.theiropportunity.com/indigenoushockeyequipmentdrive

5

Home Away from Home

Michelle and Brian Reid

Michelle and Brian Reid with one of their billets

Michelle Reid

We are lifelong hockey fans and we've been a hockey billet family since 2012. Billets provide homes for hockey players who live far from home. We live in the Windsor suburb of Tecumseh, Ontario, in a nice, quiet area, and close to downtown, where the Spitfires play. We love to go see their games.

Over the years, we've had maybe seventeen kids from various countries, plus we will keep players for other families' vacations, hockey camps, etc. These young players come to live with us while they play for the OHL Windsor Spitfires, and we've enjoyed having every one of them share our home. When a new player comes to stay with us, we tell his parents we are an extension of them, that their son will be loved, and we will look after everything. And we talk about how we run things. I will say this, being a good billet family takes patience.

We didn't set out to be a billet family. Our son played minor hockey, and then some rep hockey, so we were familiar with the concept. It was too much travelling for him though, so he went back to house league.

Our daughter Amanda used to be the game-day host for the Spitfires. She interviewed players and fans. She conducted game-day activities around the arena during games. She also made appearances as required. That is when we were first asked about possibly being a billet family by past coaches of the Spitfires, Bob Boughner and Bob Jones and Warren Rychel.

We didn't feel it was the right time for us, especially when we still had a sixteen-year-old daughter living at home. But we thought maybe down the road, when she moves out, we would consider it. Sure enough, when she went away to university, we started the process of becoming a billet family.

We started talking to the Spitfires' coaches about it. Just a couple of weeks later, we had our first player move in with us. Just before, Brian remembers being in the United States on business. The Spitfires' video coach, Jerrod Smith, called him up and said, "Hey Brian, we have a kid, and he needs a home." He told him he needed to call his wife and talk about it first and discuss it. Our son was still living at home. We made that decision to billet a player within one day.

Eric Diodati arrived at our house on a Tuesday. He showed up with a green garbage bag full of clothes and a suit on a hanger and introduced himself. Brian looked at him and said, "Hi, I'm Brian. I guess you're living with us now!"

We sat outside with Eric by our backyard barbeque area, and we had a good talk. We said, "We are new at this, and you have to help us out. We have never done this before and we have no clue what goes on." Eric was nineteen when he moved in with us. He had just come from the Mississauga Steelheads. Eric was a really great kid, and he gave us a blueprint for what to do and what not to do as billets, giving us tips. To this day, Eric tells us it was the best year he had in hockey, and he loves us.

We ended up becoming really good friends with his parents. We even went camping with them one summer and we continue to stay in touch. There was a lot to learn with that first experience, but more than anything we realized that becoming a hockey billet means your family grows.

Brian Reid

The rules for a billet player are basically set in stone by the team; in our case it was the Spitfires. Being respectful of the team, being prompt to practices and games. Attending team appearances when requested and observing team curfew rules.

And we had our own rules on top of that. The players are allowed to have girls come over, but never in the bedroom. We expect the players to be respectful to us and our family. As billets, we are here to help bring up responsible young men.

If a player breaks the curfew set by the team, we're supposed to report it to the team, the coach being the primary contact. But if it was a really good kid—someone who never broke rules—and he missed curfew one time, we would handle that ourselves. We tried not to go to the team for every little thing that might happen. It all depended on the situation.

Other than that, we had our normal, everyday routine. Nothing changed for us that way. We just had an extra mouth to feed. In the 2021–2022 season, our billet was still in school, so I had to make sure lunches were made so he had something to eat and got to school on time.

Maybe the biggest duty of being a billet parent is making sure the players are properly fed. The athletic trainer meets with us at the beginning of the season and we go over the food plan for the billet. The team and the trainers give us a list of the basic foods and necessities for the player to get through the season and excel as an athlete. We feed them a lot of fruit and vegetables and make sure they stay hydrated. On top of that, the team will tell us if the player is on any medication, and we have to make sure they are taking the right ones. If a player gets a cold and runs out to a local pharmacy, the team wants us to make sure he doesn't get the wrong cough medicine.

The players are old enough to know when to take their medicine. Brian and I conducted simple check-ins with them just to make sure, and the players always appreciated that.

Other than that, we stay in close contact with the trainer throughout the season in case any questions do come up from the team.

After being a billet for a number of years, we've learned to pre-plan meals to keep ahead of everything. That way, we know basically what we are eating for almost every night through the season. But junior hockey players are still kids, and if a Sunday night rolls around and they have an off-night from the rink, we all have some pizza.

We figured out how to be billets with Eric, but after he left there was a whole new learning curve to go through. Eric was an overage player and could pretty well take care of himself. Our next player was a fifteen-year-old Russian who had come to Canada to play hockey. Daniil Vertiy was going to be the baby of the team that year. He knew some English when he arrived, and he was well climatized to North America. But we had to teach him some more English. He was a little nervous when he came into our house, but we did well with him. We continue to stay in touch to this day.

We try to always keep an open discussion with the players. We feel that helps them deal with being away from home. It is hard for the players, especially when they are so far from home, in a different country—and thank God for FaceTime. With the new technology they can talk a lot with their family. Still, the grind of the season can get to some players. It seems to hit hardest around mid-November. We try to stay positive every day and talk about it with them. It's important to us that our house isn't just a roof over their heads. It should also be a safe place for them to be themselves, and talk freely, if they want to. Young players may not want to open up to their coaches or teammates, especially if they think they'll be looked down on for any reason: for missing home, for not feeling at ease in their new environment, for struggling with anything at all. And while FaceTime is great, it can't fully replace the comfort that's possible when you sit down face-to-face with someone who cares.

Every kid we've had live with us was awesome in their own way, and we have a special bond with each one. But some are a bit more special and stand out.

With Mikhail Sergachev, it was tough at first because when he came from Russia, he knew no English at all. He was a young guy coming to a foreign land and he didn't know anybody. The Spitfires assigned him to us and said, "Here you go!" It was up to us to figure it out. At first, Vertiy was still living with us, which of course helped a lot. Then he got traded to North Bay, and suddenly Mikhail was all by himself in a house after that.

Michelle

I don't know why, but we really hit it off. That year I didn't work, I stayed home with him. That helped a lot as well. We would have dinner as a family in the evenings. I was with him during the day, and after lunch I would get him at the rink, and we would talk. Thank goodness for Google Translate!

These young kids are a sponge; they learn things so quickly. The difference with Mikhail, as opposed to some other players who come from overseas, is that he really wanted to learn English. It is all up to the player, how badly they want to learn the language. Mikhail put in a lot of work on his own. He would watch English TV shows and documentaries to help him. His goal was to go to the show, and he knew that learning English is what he needed to do.

Whenever Mikhail was in our home and he didn't understand something, he would ask us, and we would explain it to him. Once we told him, he would retain it. We'd say all the time, "If you are going to make mistakes, make the mistakes with us here at home." By winter he was able to say a lot more in English. He was comfortable from the first day he stayed with us. His English grew better each day. We worked with him every day to help him gain the confidence he needed to be able to speak to the other boys on the team and to the coaches.

At the beginning, Mikhail struggled to make friends because of the language barrier. After a few months, things got better, and he made some friends.

Mikhail got a lot of one-on-one time with us that first year. He didn't go home to Russia for Christmas, so he spent the holidays with us. After the Christmas break, we were able to get his parents to come from Russia for a visit. They came to our house, and we celebrated New Year's Eve together. His parents coming for a visit helped him a lot that first year in Windsor.

Mikhail is a great person, and we have become even tighter over the years. He worked very, very hard to get to where he is today, a longtime member of the Tampa Bay Lightning. When I think of him the first night he got dropped off at our house, and then to see where he is now, with two Stanley Cup rings, he has grown *so* much. It makes us feel good that we did something for that kid.

Other players who have lived with us have enjoyed success after they left the Spitfires. Sean Day plays for the Syracuse Crunch, the Tampa Bay Lightning's AHL farm team. We talked to Sean before he left for Lightning training camp in 2021 and told him, "It is all up to you whether you make it." These kids know it's a hard road, but they're all so driven. We have a couple of kids who are playing in the KHL (Kontinental Hockey League) now.

Brian

For the most part, the kids living with us know what they are here for. This is their chance to play pro hockey. You have to do the best you can, or you won't make it. Ninety-five percent of the kids that have been in our house, they know they need their sleep, and they have their nap in the afternoon. They wake up at 3:10 in the afternoon on a game day and have their meal and then relax before going to the rink. It is very regimented.

Michelle

But when it comes to eating food, it is almost nonstop with these kids. We get money towards food for the player. It is not a large amount; you don't do this to make money. There were a few that could eat massive amounts of food! They would eat almost every kind of vegetable we would feed them. For the most part, none of our players were picky. One of them might not like Brussels sprouts, but they would eat everything else. These are healthy kids, and they know they need a lot of good food to succeed. We learn what they like and make sure it is available for them. Though, we might make them a smoothie with something good in there that they have no clue about!

While they all share the same dedication to taking care of themselves and doing as the team instructs, each kid is different, of course. Mostly, the kids are pretty outgoing, but some are very quiet. Even the quiet ones, though, open up after a while. We are a very personable family, and the kids seem to gravitate to us. It doesn't take long for us to start having good talks together.

The players know that when they speak with us, it stays within our family. Knowing that helps the players open up about their feelings or any situations they might have going on in their lives. They know that we have their back.

Brian

Players have highs and they have lows, and you have to deal with that. We just had our first experience billeting a goalie. My gosh, that was tough—it's so hard for goalies. We would tell him that he played a good game, but when the team loses, even when he plays well, what does everyone do? They blame the goalie. Even when it isn't his fault, the goalie gets too much of the blame. And they put a lot of pressure on themselves. He was a good kid and we loved having him.

Michelle

We've learned the key to being a good billet is communication. You also need patience, and you have to have the time to do the job well. It definitely isn't something that you go into to make money.

There is work involved and a lot of planning throughout the season. And the kids don't look after themselves, because they can't yet. They need support, and they need a family, even the overagers. When they are seventeen, or eighteen, or nineteen years old, they all think they are mature. But they are still young guys, and they need guidance. We always say that our job is to help bring up respectable young adults.

Brian

The nineteen-year-olds are allowed to go out and get a drink, because they are the legal drinking age in Ontario. Every once in a while, the team will give these players a "green light" night with a later curfew than they are used to. The players know what they can and cannot do. It has certainly been our experience that they behave.

It isn't all work being a billet. The team gives us tickets to games, and that is a big perk. We still love going to see the Spitfires play. And it isn't often that we have to drive the players anywhere. There are usually enough overage players who drive, and they make plans so that every-one gets picked up.

Because of Covid, a lot of players were not able to get their driver's licence. In the 2021–2022 season the Spitfires were short of drivers, so Brian needed to drive some players to the rink.

Covid was so disruptive to hockey. We were in a good routine, billeting players and living our lives around the Spitfires season, when Covid hit in 2020. It was early March and there were still games left to play in the season. It was a Thursday, March 12, that the boys left for the rink for a game. They were back in just over a half an hour. The season was cancelled, and the players were told to pack up.

We had two players from Finland who were billeting with us. They were both scrambling to get home. Finland was shutting their borders down and we had to get them to the airport as soon as possible so they could get back into their own country. We never thought that Covid would go on as long as it did. We were so happy for the start of the 2021–2022 season. We needed it, we all needed hockey back. Seeing sports again gives us back our normal, and it gives us a little hope. Even if we are wearing a mask and have to show our proof of vaccinations. And we missed having people in our lives.

We spoke earlier about Mikhail Sergachev and what he means to our family. In spring 2021, the Tampa Bay Lightning were at the Bell Centre in Montreal for game 3 and game 4 of the Stanley Cup Final. Mikhail asked us to come, so we did. To be in the rink and to see fans there—it is hard to describe how good it felt seeing fans. It smelled like hockey in there and it was so emotional. Watching Mikhail play over twenty minutes in a Stanley Cup Final game would have been special no matter what, but the whole experience reminded us of what we'd been missing, and why we do this work.

Being a good billet family is a constant learning process. Every player is different, and we recognize that. We try to establish a good relationship with the kids and try to be very open with them. We give them respect, and they give it to us.

Michelle

I know some people won't believe us, but we had all great experiences as billet parents. Now, every kid is different, and some of them come to us from different countries, and sometimes English isn't their first language. We enjoy billeting players from different countries; we feel it brings a different light into our family.

We love being billet parents.

6

In It for the Long Haul

Jason Payne

© Tony Bailey Photography

E veryone in hockey gets a nickname, usually by adding or taking away a few letters from your name and adding an "er" or "y" at the end. For me, Payne became "Payner." But my best friend in hockey, and in life, former NHL goalie Kevin Weekes, gave me another name: "Stayner." As much as hockey wanted to get rid of me, I was like a stain that wouldn't go away. And I love hockey way too much to ever go away.

Like a lot of kids, I fell in love with the game early on. My mom is from St. Lucia, but I was born and raised in Toronto. The first time I went skating, my parents took me to St. Mike's Arena, near our first house at Bathurst and St. Clair. I enjoyed it right away. It wasn't long after that I started playing hockey. The more I played the more everything clicked. I was a goalie for most of my childhood; I only switched to forward when I was going into Minor Bantam, when I was thirteen years old.

We had moved to North York after grade four, and I played house league at the Cummer Park Arena, close to our new home in the Finch and Leslie area of North York. My older brother was coaching a house league team in Oriole Park, in the Don Valley area. He called me one day and asked me if I wanted to play for his team. I played goalie for him. There were no free passes for family though—he worked me hard. My brother said, "I am going to make you the best goalie in the league!" I had no idea what he meant by that at first, but I found out. By the end of the season, I won the goalie of the year award for our house league. It was a lot of fun and I made friends I still talk to today.

Over time, I had many friends playing at a high level of rep hockey. (One of them was Kevin; he and I grew up in the same neighbourhood in Bathurst and St. Clair.) Entering my Minor Bantam year, my dad said to me, "I know you are a goalie, but you should try to be a player. You have a better chance of making it as a player." I thought, sure, why not?

That summer I went to a hockey camp at Seneca College. I had to borrow my friend's gear because all I had at the time was goalie equipment. Former NHLer and two-time Stanley Cup champion Adam Graves was one of the main instructors at the camp, and he was great. It was a fun camp, and I was able to learn a lot. Just watching Graves and how he moved on the ice and watching him shoot the puck was a big influence on me. That camp had an immediate impact on me and it inspired me to work on the skills I needed as a player as opposed to what it takes to be a goalie.

After that, I had different skills to work on, and I took every chance to get on the ice. I played shinny and pickup hockey—I even played ball hockey—and continued to plug away at playing forward. I tried out for some teams, and I didn't make them, but that didn't stop me. At first, my slap shot wasn't very good. I could do it in ball hockey, but when I got on the ice, I couldn't get the hang of it. But I kept working on my shot until it took off. People may not know this, but ball hockey is a great way to work on your skills. Stick-handling a ball helps your ability to stick-handle a puck. It also helps your hand-eye coordination, which is an important skill in hockey. I learned a lot of my hockey skills playing ball hockey and street hockey.

One day, when I was thirteen, I went to play shinny in Scarborough and there was a team practicing after us. One of the coaches saw me and he asked me my age, and so I told him. Then he asked if I was playing anywhere. I told him I wasn't, and he invited me to practice with his team, the Toronto Devils, then an A-level team. I was always up for more hockey; I even still had my gear on. It was great feeling being asked to play for them. We had fun and everyone got along so well. For me, it wasn't hard at all fitting in. Everyone could see that I was driven, I had a good work ethic, and I had the right personality to fit in with everyone. After the practice he invited me to join the team. It was a great experience, and I learned a lot. It introduced me to hockey at the rep level as a forward. The experience drove me to want to play AA and AAA like a lot of my friends. Some of those friends didn't think I was good enough to play forward at that level, but I had my own vision of what I wanted to achieve. But it wasn't easy.

I tried out for an AA team, the Hillcrest Summits, and didn't make it, so I continued playing A. But they stayed in contact with me and allowed me to practice with them. The Summits played out of Cummer Park Arena, just around the corner from my house in North York. Whenever I had a day from my A team and the Summits were practicing, I would skate with them. I was (and still am) grateful the coach gave me that opportunity to keep working on my skills.

I was on the ice at least five days of the week, and it kept me very busy. Later on, when I was coaching, I would tell the kids, "Stay busy, stay active, and stay in sports." You don't want that idle time, which is where you find yourself in trouble. There are always outside influences that can lead a child down the wrong path. My mother made sure I was involved in a lot of sports. She wanted me to be active and involved in a good environment. My mom made it a point while I was growing up to keep me busy. I was in swimming, soccer, baseball—you name it—and I'm forever thankful for that.

All the extra practice paid off when, the next year, the coach of the Summits asked me to join the team. Not even a year after switching from goalie to forward, I was playing AA during my Major Bantam year.

Going into my Minor Midget year, I tried out for a number of AAA teams. I almost made the Toronto Red Wings, but I was one of the final cuts. I went back and played AA for Hillcrest, but my hunger and desire to play AAA, to get to the next level, never left me. I called up one of the coaches for the Wexford Raiders AAA team. He allowed me to try out for the team in mid-season. Nobody thought I was good enough to play AAA, but I went out and made the team! All those coaches who didn't think I was good enough just gave me the fuel to prove them wrong. I used that fuel every day to reach my goal.

Now, to be honest, I wasn't a star player for the Raiders. Some games I only played a few shifts, and that taught me a hard lesson. When you only play a few shifts in a game, that is tough to take. But it was a good lesson for me to learn. I learned to never take anything for granted, nothing is given, it is only earned. All that taught me to play every shift like it was my last.

But I was where I wanted to be. I stuck to it and after that season I went to my first OHL, Ontario Hockey League, training camp, in Owen Sound. I had a great time, but I knew I wasn't ready to play at the OHL level. I came back home and played Major Midget AAA with the Mississauga Senators. We had a good year and ended up going far in the playoffs. But I was already looking ahead again to the next level: the OHL. That was my next goal.

Later that summer, when the playoffs were over, I went to the OHL Sault Ste. Marie Greyhounds training camp and made it all the way to the final cuts. I didn't make the team, but it was progress. I bounced around a few places after that. I travelled out west and went to training camp with the Tri-City Americans of the Western Hockey League. That didn't work out, and next I attended a camp with the Seattle Thunderbirds. Later on, I tried out for a team in the Quebec League (QMJHL). Even though I was cut by all these teams, I gained valuable experience, and I was meeting people in the game. I felt that each stop along the way I was getting a little better and getting closer to my goal. I even played a little junior in the Saskatchewan Junior Hockey League (SJHL). I also learned a lot just travelling across Canada the way that I did. Though hockey, I was able to see a lot of different parts of Canada. I was fortunate enough to attend training camps with three leagues in the Canadian Hockey League: the WHL, the OHL, and the QMJHL. It certainly gave me a unique perspective of hockey at all different levels in the different communities across Canada. What I did learn was that the style of hockey is different from the WHL, to the OHL, and to the QMJHL. All of it helped teach me how to adapt to different styles of hockey.

When I wasn't attending camps (or playing briefly in Saskatchewan) I was playing high school football back in Toronto, at Victoria Park. I was an all-star football player and I had just got back from camp in the Soo. We were playing a game when someone blocked me low and rolled up on my ankle. I heard something pop. That ended my game and most of the season. Four days later I received a phone call from the Newmarket Royals OHL team. They wanted me to come out for a try-out. I had my ankle immersed in a bucket of ice water, trying to get the swelling down. I almost got frostbite trying to heal my ankle! I taped it up the best I could in Newmarket, but that injury was too much for me to handle.

That was another big lesson, one I passed on to kids when I was coaching AAA so they wouldn't have to learn it the hard way: if it's your OHL draft year, you need to focus only on hockey.

When I finally made it to junior, I was playing for the London Knights. I was playing with a Junior B team in North York called the Royal York Rangers. Ten games into the season I received a phone call from a buddy of mine, Roy Gray, who played for the Knights. He said the team needed help, and he thought I could fit right in. I hopped on a Greyhound bus the next day to go to London and attend practice. After practice, the coach, Mike Fedorko, looked at me and asked me if I wanted to sign with the team. I think that was one of the happiest days in my life. I had accomplished a goal that I'd been trying to achieve: I was playing in the OHL.

I was getting serious about what it took to make it. The lessons I'd learned and the experiences I'd had were all adding up.

When I started playing for the Knights, things were great. I was fighting and fitting in with the team and the fans loved me. Fighting was just a part of who I was. I think it is something that was just in me. I had to fight for every inch along the way, so it only seemed fitting that I would fight in hockey. However, I knew that I couldn't just rely on fighting, so I worked on other parts of my game as well. Every summer, I studied PowerSkating and trained with a skating guru in Boston by the name of Paul Vincent. Skating is such a key element in hockey and the game just keeps getting faster and more skilled. I had to work hard on my skating to make sure that I could keep up with the play at that level. I was always told, "If you can't skate, you can't play!"

I had first met Paul when I attended the Seattle Thunderbirds training camp. Paul and his dad invited me to Boston to train with them for the summer. Paul's father is well known in the hockey world and training with them was a real education.

The gym was in Boston, but we lived in Cape Cod. Mr. Vincent would wake up at 3:30 in the morning and drive two hours into Boston. If we left any later, we would get caught in Boston's brutal rush-hour traffic. We would start training in the gym at six, and we would stop just before eleven. Then we would drive back out to the Cape and have some lunch. From there we went to the rink to work on our skating and any other skills, too.

After that, we rested a bit. Then we would do a secondary workout, running on the beach or in the water. We would be in chest-high water, running back and forth. It wasn't until later that I realized there are sharks in the water off of Cape Cod!

Mr. V was strict, and he taught me how to conduct myself, how to carry myself. One of the best lessons he taught me was to surround yourself with like-minded people who strive to succeed. That summer, my friends were home and wanted to go out and have fun, while I was a long way from home, working hard. You need the right environment to reach your goals and to this day, I still send him messages, thanking him for teaching me this. One of those like-minded people is one of the rocks in my life, Kevin Weekes.

Throughout my hockey journey, I had transferred from school to school. Because of that, my education suffered. When I was going to school in London, I had to work harder to get caught up in my classes.

Tuesday night was movie night for the team and so our curfew was a little later. One Tuesday, after a movie, I came home to my billet house. My billets sent the coach a message telling him that I was going out late at night, and I wasn't doing that at all. I never drank and I never did anything crazy in those days. Why my billet parents wouldn't talk to me first is a question that still baffles me. I never drank or did drugs, that isn't a part of my personality, and it isn't who I am. I got along with everyone. I kept my mouth shut and kept working and playing.

Shortly afterwards, I had an assignment due in order to catch up to the rest of the class. I had to write a paper on *Frankenstein* by Mary Shelley. I stayed up until two in the morning in the living room of my billets' house, finishing my paper. I got it done, I was happy, and I handed it in the next day.

When I showed up to practice after school, my locker stall was empty. The trainer, Grant, came up to me, and said, "The coach wants to see you." I walked into the coach's office, and he said, "Your billets have been complaining that you are up all night and you went out partying and you didn't come home until three in the morning."

I was stunned. I told him I'd stayed up until two in the morning writing the paper on *Frankenstein*. He didn't want to hear what I had to say. "That's it," he said, "we are done, and we are going to send you home." One of the assistant coaches took me to my billets' house and watched me collect my belongings. Then he took me down to the bus terminal and put me on a bus back to Toronto. That was the longest bus ride of my life. The whole way home, I replayed the events in my head, knowing that I did nothing wrong. But it didn't matter.

The whole thing upset me so much. I knew I didn't do anything wrong. Maybe they thought they were doing the right thing. I really don't know. But it felt like they were trying to crush my dream, and it was tough.

The funny thing is, my relationship with my coaches seemed fine. But as you find out later in life, especially in the position that I am in now, people take information and act before getting the whole story from both sides. I took the whole experience in London as one big life lesson.

I stayed focused the best I could, and I kept working. I started the next season in Utica, New York, in the Colonial League as a twenty-year-old. This was like the movie *Slap Shot.* I ended up with 85 penalty minutes in only 14 games. I was fighting guys seven and eight years older than me. By the Christmas break, I knew I still wanted to play in the OHL, and at my age I only had one last chance.

I contacted the Barrie Colts. Bert Templeton was as old school as they come and he wanted me because in London, I was known as a fighter. He gave me a chance to play. He was a tough man and drove us all hard. One day I walked into the rink and my locker stall was empty. Our assistant coach said to me, "Bert is sending you home." I couldn't believe it. "He is sending me home for what? What did I do? Where is Bert?"

He had just left. I ran outside the arena and spotted him getting into his car as quick as he could. I was yelling at him to get his attention, but he drove away. I couldn't believe it. That was the end of my OHL career.

The next year, I went back to the Colonial League, this time playing for Flint. That is where my pro career really started to take off. I spent the entire year with the organization, but I was also called up to play in the IHL and the AHL. I was called up to Carolina in the AHL. They were the farm team of the NHL Florida Panthers at the time. Kevin Weekes was playing for the Panthers, and I was able to spend some time with him. Kevin has always been a best friend. Every time we're on the phone, the call lasts a minimum of forty-five minutes. I was so grateful to have this time to connect in person. We'd come a long way from our rep hockey days in North Toronto, but I still had a big goal in front of me. Kevin Weekes has been my rock throughout my whole career, he has always been beside me, supporting me. All through junior and pro hockey his message to me was "Keep grinding." He would tell me, "Keep grinding, act like a pro, train like a pro, and you will be a pro."

Eventually I moved over to the East Coast Hockey League with a friend of mine, Greg Ireland; he'd coached me when I was with the Dayton Bombers. Greg pushed me to where I needed to be. He really helped me understand a part of the game that not many people can figure out: mental toughness. I have dealt with it throughout my career to that point: to understand it, to analyze it, and then to overcome it as a tool. Learning that helped me continue to push. The game of hockey can definitely put a mental strain on anybody. Hockey wants to give you every opportunity to hang them up and quit. It can be very unforgiving at times. By being strong mentally, it gave me another skill set. Greg Ireland made me truly understand who I was as a player, and as a person. And mental toughness is a skill that helped survive the grind of the ECHL. I fought well-known tough guys like Jody Shelley and Darin Kimble. It was my job, and I had to do my job.

I ended up playing for twenty-five teams in six leagues over fourteen years of pro hockey. I tell players this: hockey gives you every opportunity to quit and walk away from the game. Playing pro hockey is not for the weak of heart and it requires resilience. I love the game and I believed in myself and what I could do. I kept plugging away, even though there were times when things were not good. One year, I was traded four times during that season. At one point I did say, "What am I doing? Is this for me?" But I kept pushing and kept travelling around, looking for the best opportunities.

Typically, I would get anywhere from $700 to $1,000 a week. I certainly never made $50,000 in a single season at any point during my pro career.

Looking back on my hockey-playing career, I wouldn't change anything. Would I have liked to have stuck in one place longer? Yes, of course I would. Would I have liked to have made the teams that I was cut from? Yes, of course. But all of the trials and tribulations that I went through, they have molded me into the player that I was, and the coach that I am today.

None of it came easily. Being Black, throughout my playing career I have heard racist chirps from opposing players on numerous occasions. But I'm a fighter, and if guys wanted to say that stuff to me, I had no problem because they had to answer to me on the ice.

As for fans, I'd hear it from them sometimes, too, but I'd never let them get to me. That's what they wanted, to get under my skin, throw me off my game. It happened to me in the OHL, and it happened to me in pro hockey. I always found the best thing to do is not let them think it bothers you. I would always laugh along and let it go. The more you show them it's getting to you, the more you encourage them to say racist things. Even when it bothers you, you have to stay strong and focused on what you need to do.

I always tried to carry myself as the best teammate I could be.

One game when I played pro, we were at the end of a shootout. The opposing player missed his shot, and our whole team chirped him for not scoring. He looked directly at me and called me the N-word three times. I wasn't even on the ice. My whole team lost it. The linesman was standing between the benches, and he skated over and said, "Don't worry, I saw it."

When the shootout was done, I was the last guy off the bench. All of my teammates had already jumped off the bench and went after that guy! I realized something at that moment: He said that to me and I was still on the bench. And the rest of my team was going after that guy. They were doing it for me, and it was a great sign that the team had my back. From then on, I always made sure I had everyone else's back, too. It is unfortunate the way the world is. You have to keep fighting the good fight, and it helps when you have a team around you.

As soon I was done playing pro hockey, I got into coaching, and it was because of a friendship made years before that I had that opportunity. My final year of pro hockey, I was with the Reading Royals of the ECHL. (I finished the season with the Wheeling Nailers.) The coach in Reading was Jason Nobili, whom I've known since I was kid. When I was playing AAA for the Mississauga Senators, Jason's younger brother was my teammate.

My mother never drove, so I would always take the subway to get to games back then. I would go to Wilson Station, and Jason's dad would pick me up and drive us to the rink in Mississauga.

In Reading, as I was winding down my pro career, Jason was helping me transition to the coaching role. I was basically his player/assistant coach at the time.

The same time I retired as a player, Jason decided to come back home and started coaching the AAA Junior Canadiens in Toronto. I had just started working in Loss Prevention at the Bay in downtown Toronto. There aren't a lot of career options for recently retired athletes. Another price you pay for pursuing that dream. But then Jason called me up one day and asked if I wanted to coach with him. I said yes right away, and I quit my job at the Bay.

I coached AAA with Jason for around two years. I then moved to Kingston and started a new job as a scout and skills and skating coach for the OHL Frontenacs. That lasted one year, and then I moved back to Toronto. I enjoyed being a skills coach. But dealing with the politics that I had dealt with before during my time in junior hockey was not something that I wanted to do. So I moved back to Toronto and started coaching the AAA Mississauga Senators. I started out coaching the 1997 birth-year team, but then they offered me a chance to coach a group of players over that in age by a number of years. That would have been in 2013, and I started coaching the 2002 birth-year Pee Wee team. I was a little nervous at first. I wasn't sure if I wanted to coach kids that young. But I decided I could do it well, so when I said yes, I made a vow that I was going to be committed to these kids. I wanted the challenge, but I also did it to better understand what kids these days are taught and what makes them tick. These kids are part of the "Why Generation": they all want to know why. I don't think kids are bad, they are just misled or misunderstood. The job of a good coach is connecting with your players and helping them navigate through life and through sports.

Now, if the kids were bad sometimes, the parents could be even worse! Some parents just didn't know any better, and every parent thinks their kid is the best player on the team. Dealing with parents was always an issue in minor hockey. But as long as you had good communication and you were genuine and authentic, then they could never question my intentions. They all knew that I only wanted what was best for their children. I coached that group of kids all the way up to Minor Midget. I wasn't just learning how to coach, I had to learn how players are recruited by other teams in the Greater Toronto Hockey League. The first two weeks of the season is bliss, but it is recruiting season for AAA players in the GTHL. We would get to November, with the team coming together, and I would have players being recruited to play for other teams. I couldn't believe it.

One year, going into Bantam, I had some pretty talented players. Here I was, developing these kids, and a number of other teams recruited them out from under me. That was a tough year, and we didn't make the playoffs. But that experience prepared me for Minor Midget. I recruited hard and I assembled a good group of kids. I knew they would work hard and I believed in them.

I had a meeting with the parents where I said to them, "We are in Minor Midget now. This is their OHL draft year. The biggest part of this season is making it to the OHL Cup. If we do that, it gives everyone better exposure to junior scouts. Do you want me to do whatever I have to do to get us there, or do you want me to play everyone equally, rolling the lines, whether it helps us win or not?" All the parents said, "We want to go to the Cup!" I did what I had to do that year and, as a team, we reached our goal.

There were some parents that were not happy because their kids didn't get a lot of ice time. But what's best for a team isn't necessarily fair to each player—at least not at first. We were a middle-of-the-pack team that made it to the OHL Cup, and afterwards we had more players drafted off our team than some of the top-ranked teams that finished above us in the standings. I'm sure some of the parents weren't as keen on the plan to start with, but a handful thanked me after the season for getting us there.

Learning how to cope with the criticisms and doubts, and

manage people's expectations, helped prepare me for when I started coaching pro hockey. It also helped that when I got to the pro level, a lot of the players I saw in the ECHL were players that I had coached in AAA hockey. The big difference was not having to deal with parents anymore. I tell my players today that if they have problems with their ice time or something else that is going on, they are grown men and can come talk to me. Hockey is a team sport and based on relationships.

And who and where I coach today is totally different. Early in my career, I played a short stint with St. Michael's College School in Toronto and one of my teammates was Matt Thomas. Matt ended up playing in the NCAA and got into coaching while I was in the midst of my pro hockey career. Later on, Matt was coaching at the University of Alaska–Anchorage, and he was watching my Toronto Patriots team of the Ontario Junior Hockey League (OJHL) to recruit players. Matt and I were talking on a regular basis, and I would give him updates on players that he should look at. Not long afterwards, I was at the Ripley Aquarium in Toronto with my family. My phone buzzed and there was a text message from Matt. It was right to the point: "Hey, would you be interested in coaching down in Cincinnati with me?" The Cincinnati Cyclones are part of the Buffalo Sabres organization, so this could be a big step. I showed Ashley, my wife, the text. She said, "You better go find out what is going on and what that is all about."

I was wandering around Ripley's looking for a good cell signal and finally got ahold of Matt. He told me he just got the job as the head coach of the Cyclones. He described the job he was offering and the pay and everything else. It wasn't much money, no more than I was making at the time with various things going on. However, he was offering me a step towards my dream and my goal and that was more important. About two weeks later, he officially offered me the job.

I was an assistant coach of the Cyclones for two seasons, sometimes dealing with the front office of the Sabres organization, but usually we were able to do our own thing. Then at the start of the 2021–2022 season, Matt got a job with the Providence Bruins of the AHL. The next thing I knew, I was being offered the job to be the head coach of the Cyclones.

When Cyclones general manager Kristin Ropp called me, she set up a meeting to finalize everything. I said to her, "I would be honoured. But just understand what is going to happen now. When this gets out, this story is going to attract a lot of attention." I am a person of colour, coaching pro hockey.

I still remember riding the bus with the Cyclones when I was an assistant coach and Kevin Weekes would give us a shout-out on the NHL Network (he became a broadcaster after retiring from pro hockey). Now this was happening. As I predicted, the story took off and I went through numerous interviews. It brought a lot of attention to hockey and that is good for the sport. I am pleased it happened, and I am going to continue to do my best. I have to say, working for the Cincinnati Cyclones has been nothing but an amazing experience and journey in my career. The organization embraces the concept that hockey is for everyone. It doesn't matter if you are a person of colour, or if you are a different gender. The focus is on having great people in the organization and that is all that matters. Our general manager, Kristin Ropp, is one of only a handful of female GMs in pro hockey. She is one of the best.

We have passionate fans here in Cincinnati, and they want our team to do well. The reality is that things are not always going to go the way everyone wants. My job is to fight through the down times and not get too low or high. There are always positive takeaways from a season and areas to work on improving. But coaching is mostly about people and those relationships.

If there is one thing I can do it is relate to players in the minors, and players who spend a lot of time on the bench. I had a conversation one morning with a player on the Cyclones because he was frustrated by how much time he was sitting on the bench. I wanted to change his perspective. I said to him, "The problem is, you are worrying about things that you can't control. I have been through this, so I understand. I have been in games where I played the first shift of the game and fought. And I didn't see the ice again until the very last shift of the game."

It's hard to watch your teammates battle out there while you do nothing, so your perspective can make all the difference. I continued, "My attitude was, I am being paid, and this is my job. I just have to make sure I am ready when I am called upon. It is the coach's decision whether or not I play. My job is to just be ready."

The hardest part of hockey is the mental side. As a player, they always tell you that at least 80 percent of the game in mental, and they are right. The minute your mind wanders, your body can't react. If you develop a losing mindset and feel sorry for yourself, nothing will work for you.

I understand what that feeling is like. It isn't easy to find that inner spark of motivation, so I have to find out what makes them go, what fires them up. Is it something I can say, or is it how I say it? I want the players to understand that I believe in them, and I believe in what they can do. Let's get it going, I tell them. Whatever they need, I am there to help. As a coach the challenge is finding that fine balance of patting guys on the back and driving them hard. I want my players to understand that I care, and I will go to the wall for them. But I am also fair, and I will hold everyone accountable.

It helps that my family loves Cincinnati, and it has become a second home for us. It is a great city to live in with some great people. Everyone here is warm and welcoming. Cincinnati a small "big league" city. The Cincinnati Reds are next door to us, and the Cincinnati Bengals are just down the street.

And the Sabres organization has been great to me, too. I spent time in Buffalo during the Sabres training camp in 2021, and Don Granato and the coaching staff are excellent. Don was my coach in the AHL when I played in Worcester. And the Sabres GM, Kevyn Adams, was a teammate of Kevin Weekes's in Carolina. It's a small world, and everyone, from Don to Kevyn and the Pegula family (ownership) all made us feel so welcome. When I first got the job offer, Jason Botterill, the Sabres' GM at the time, called me up to congratulate me. That meant a lot.

I hope the fact that I am a person of colour coaching a pro hockey team inspires others. For people coming up now, it's important to see somebody they can relate to in a position of success. That recognition matters. There are more now than ever—there's even an NHL coaches association BIPOC program. The program was started a few years ago by Lindsay Pennal and Michael Hirshfeld. They have done a great job of opening doors for coaches from a variety of genders and ethnic backgrounds. There are new coaches of different colours and racial backgrounds. There are great female coaches, too. They have created a platform for everybody to network and build relationships. Lindsay and Michael are doing a great job and it is only going to keep growing.

I just hope that coaches of colour see me, and it gives them hope that they can achieve their goals. I also think of the kids coming to the game and seeing someone behind the bench that looks like them. That is an important message to send and receive in the hockey world.

One day, I will be looked at as just a coach, not a Black coach. I would love for that to happen.

Until then, we need to open the door for more people to have the opportunity to get into the game. One thing's for sure: I am in it for the long haul. Hockey can't get rid of me.

7

The Hockey Visionary

Kelly Serbu

I can understand why parents with young kids who are visually impaired feel that hockey is not an option. And there are a lot of parents in that situation. I want to change that feeling. I want to get as many people involved in blind hockey as possible.

That probably sounds dangerous, and it's often a concern at first. When I meet one of these parents, I tell them, "Don't be afraid, your child will be fine, and they won't get seriously hurt. A kid will get bumps and bruises whether they are visually impaired or not." I've played the game with good vision and deteriorating vision; I have received more than my share of bumps and bruises along the way, and I turned out just fine.

Growing up, I was a military brat. My dad joined the Canadian Armed Forces when he was nineteen years old. My dad was young, and he wanted to see the world. My family is from Alberta, and Dad, a Romanian, grew up in a farming town. My mom is English and Métis. My dad is from Willingdon, Alberta. In 1965 he was stationed in Halifax. That year he went back home to Edmonton on leave. He met my mother while he was there. My mom is from Edmonton and the two met at a party. After that, she decided to move out to Halifax to be with my dad. At the time, dad was a gunner on the HMCS *Bonaventure*, the Canadian Navy's last aircraft carrier.

This was in the late sixties. When the Canadian government decommissioned the *Bonny*, my dad decided to re-muster to a different trade in the military. He became a clearance diver, one of the most physically demanding jobs in the navy. It's the Canadian version of an underwater demolition/navy frogman that you see in the movies. He did that work for over thirty years and reached the highest noncommission rank in the Canadian Navy, chief petty officer first class. He retired at the age of fifty-five.

My dad is in his mid-seventies now, and he still plays hockey three days a week. When he retired, he wore the same kit (shirts, pants, etc.) that he wore when he enlisted at nineteen. It all still fit him. My dad was always in shape, and he hasn't missed a beat since retirement. He lives in Cole Harbour, Nova Scotia, and skates with the same group of guys every week.

When I was a kid, I played hockey, baseball, and ten years of soccer. I boxed, too. I tried just about every sport, but hockey was my passion. Because Dad was stationed in CFB Shearwater, just outside of Dartmouth, Nova Scotia, I also spent time paddling kayaks, and I raced in the K1 and K2 disciplines. The K1 is a one-person kayak, the K2 is a two-person. That was a blast. One of my kayak competitors at the Mic Mac kayak club in Dartmouth was longtime NHL goalie Olaf Kolzig. Although he was originally born in South Africa, Kolzig lived in Halifax during his preteen and teenage years.

I remember him playing Pee Wee, Bantam, and Midget hockey. Olaf was a year older than me, and after his Midget year in Dartmouth, he moved away to play in the WHL. Whenever he played, the parents and the fans would chant, "Holy molie, what a goalie!"

My parents instilled in me from a very young age the importance of going to university and getting an education. My first year at Saint Mary's University, I wasn't sure if I was going to play junior or university hockey. I went to one practice at Saint Mary's, and it was an eye-opener. I was skating with men.

There was one guy on the team, I will never forget him, his name was Johnny Gladiator. He had just come back from LA Kings training camp. On the ice I realized why his name was Gladiator: he was a big, strong player. I ended up getting in a fight that skate, but not with him. The next week I signed with Halifax and played junior while I went to school. I played left wing, and I was playing while at Saint Mary's in Halifax.

That was about the time I started noticing problems with my vision. I was around nineteen years old, my second year playing junior in Halifax. I noticed it more when I was driving. I got my licence when I was sixteen and I bought this little Dodge Colt for $600. I painted it myself and did everything I could to keep it on the road. But the car wasn't the issue.

My vision at night wasn't great to begin with, but soon I struggled to see things on the road. When it was raining, I couldn't see things that other people would have no trouble seeing. I would be driving my buddies and they thought I was joking around. They would tell me, "Did you see that?" after a near miss and I would try to cover up and say, "Oh yeah, I saw it." About the time I was turning twenty, there were signs that my vision, especially when I was driving, was becoming a real problem. If there was something in a construction zone that wasn't lit well, I couldn't see it, but everyone else could.

I was in my second year at Saint Mary's at this time, studying political science. I originally was studying business, then I quickly realized that wasn't for me.

The fall of 1990 was when I really started to worry. I couldn't read the board in class. I thought I just needed a new prescription for my glasses. I'd been going to the same eye doctor for years and I knew him well.

I noticed he was acting a bit differently with me on this visit. He had me do these eye exercises, following his pen, which was new. I had never done that test before. This was a doctor that I had since I was a kid. I played hockey against his son while I was growing up. Looking back, I suspect he thought whatever issue I had was something that was not good. I don't think he wanted to disappoint me and give me the bad news.

Right afterwards, he sent me for a battery of tests. I went to three different hospitals to complete all of the tests on my eyes.

Just over five months after my initial visit, in February 1991, I had another appointment with my eye doctor. My mom was with me, and we walked into the office and sat down. He looked at me and got right to the point. "Okay, you have this disease called Stargardt's. There is no treatment for it, and eventually your vision is going to get worse. By the time you are forty, you will likely be legally blind." He went on, "You can talk to people at the Canadian National Institute for the Blind for more information."

I had no clue what legally blind meant or what Stargardt was. He kept talking, but I wasn't able to absorb any of it. I had to go to hockey practice after the appointment, and I had to take my mom back to the Halifax ferry terminal.

Back then in Nova Scotia, licences didn't have a photo, it was just a piece of paper with three parts. When your license was up for renewal, you basically just signed the one section and mailed it in. There was a question that asked you to confirm that you had no medical or health condition changes. You would just answer no, sign it, and mail it in, and they sent you a new license. Later on, I met someone else who had the same eye disease as me, and he was still driving while wearing these special bifocals. Unlike me, he never stopped driving. I looked into it and checked out these bifocals and saw a doctor about it. I tried them once and said, "goodbye," and handed them back to the doctor and never tried to wear them ever again.

Nobody reported my condition to a registry of motor vehicles and the doctor didn't say anything about playing hockey. Do what you can as long as you can.

After I finished my second year of junior hockey, I told a few close buddies about my condition, but I mostly kept it quiet. I was still trying to process everything. Doctors were talking about being legally blind at forty and I was nineteen years old. I could read okay, and I thought I could deal with it.

We had a great playoff run in my second year of junior, and we advanced to the Centennial Cup. I wasn't thinking about the distant future. My last year of junior, I was still driving, and if players were from out of town, I would pick them up and take them to the rink. I liked being a go-to guy and I liked the company as I drove.

By the end of my second year of junior, I couldn't see the scoreboard clock very well, I couldn't see player numbers on the ice. As I entered my third year of junior, I really questioned my ability to drive safely.

My parents live on a cul-de-sac not far from where Sidney Crosby grew up. There were a lot of kids around. One day a thought popped into my head: *Should I be driving? What if I end up hitting somebody?* Later that summer, I was driving on a rainy night, and I hit a curb and almost had an accident. I scared myself and said, "That's it, I am not driving anymore." By early August of that summer, I decided I wasn't going to drive anymore. From then on, I would rely on my parents or my friends to get to the rink for summer skates.

Not long after I stopped driving, my mother suggested that I should go to the CNIB and see what kind of resources they had that might help me. The CNIB offices in Halifax were right across from where I played hockey at the Forum. I went in and they checked me out. Now, at this point, I just thought that my vision was bad, but I wasn't legally blind. They asked me, "Do you have your contacts in?" I said yes. They said, "Okay, there is an eye chart over there, what can you read?" I could read the giant E, and then I struggled to see anything underneath it. The gentleman that I was talking to said, "Kelly, you are legally blind." I couldn't believe it. He said, "Kelly, that is 20/200 vision, that is legally blind in Canada." I was twenty years old at the time. After I left, I started to think about what was happening to me the past year or so. We would be doing drills on the ice and the coach would be in the far corner. I would break out, skating up the left wing, and they would send a saucer pass to me. I was supposed to take the pass, and go in on net and take a shot. When the puck left the ice, I couldn't see it.

They explained that legally blind in Canada is when your vision is

20/200 or worse: that what I can see at twenty feet, someone else can see at two hundred feet. That was a big revelation about how serious a problem I had with my vision.

The CNIB gave me a bus pass and they gave me funding for some books that I needed for school. They could provide resources to help me read, but I was still struggling to get the font big enough on computers and laptops. Technology has come so far since I was diagnosed. My phone can read everything to me now.

The best thing that they gave me was an Optelec 20/20, a machine that looks like the microfiche screen from a research library. I could put a book under the Optelec and magnify the words to whatever size worked best for me. There was also a button that would switch the words from black on a white page to white letters on a black background, which sometimes helped. With the machine, I could take my time and read whatever I wanted.

Back in the early nineties, a machine like that cost at least $2,000. It was paid for through the provincial government and the CNIB. Between that and the resources available at Saint Mary's, I was better able to read my course material. The college had this group of volunteers at the school that helped a lot. If there was a book that had type too small for me to read, the volunteers would read it and record an audiobook for me. I would send them the books before the start of the course and they'd send me back an old-fashioned cassette tape. The volunteers took pride in what they did; some of them really made an effort to make the recording sound good. Maybe they wanted to be voice actors!

The recordings helped a lot, but it wasn't just my vision that was affecting my grades. In my first year at Saint Mary's, I was your typical junior hockey player and wanted to have fun with my buddies. The workload at university was a lot more than I expected, and after that first year, I was on academic probation. In my second year, I buckled down and my marks improved. But with my vision getting worse, I had to put even more time into reading and studying. By the start of my third year, I turned the switch on and said to myself, "Okay, this is my last year of junior and I want to have my best season, but I want to do the best I can academically."

At that point, I still hadn't figured out what exactly I wanted to do. I was deciding whether I would go into teaching or pursue law school. When I was playing junior hockey, as an eighteen-year-old, we had the strongest team in our league. But I was a role player and a fourth-liner. Sometimes I would move up to the top line, but I fought a lot. Bottom line: I wasn't expecting to go to the NHL. I loved hockey and I wanted to play for as long as I could. But at the same time, I knew hockey wasn't going to provide for me financially.

My plan to have a great last year of junior didn't start off well. I broke my nose before the season even began. We were in an exhibition game in Amherst, Nova Scotia. We had two guys from the OHL that were playing with us. They were not playing in the OHL anymore. They told me that I had to watch out for his guy on Amherst. I kind of thought, whatever.

This guy they were talking about was big and he'd spent time with Moncton in the AHL, at the time the Winnipeg Jets farm team. My first shift, I go down the wing, take a slap shot, and score. As I am going off the ice, this beast comes over the boards to fight me. To this day, my coach Jimbo says that he told me, "No, no!" I swear I heard him say, "Go, go!" I dropped my gloves. I landed one punch and then he busted my nose. There was blood everywhere. I had to go to the hospital for stiches. Sure enough, the guy that beat me up came in right after me with a broken hand.

Two months later, in December, right after my final exam before the holiday break at Saint Mary's, I got hurt again. We were playing a home game in Halifax Forum, and I dumped the puck in on a power play. My left hand was down by my hip as I took a hit. It wasn't a big hit, but it broke my forearm, my ulna, right through. I was out of action for the rest of December, January, and most of February.

I had tried to keep my vision problems a secret until then. My coaches knew about it, and they knew I didn't drive. Not long after the surgery to repair my arm, I was back in the rink and sitting in the seats with my parents. A local reporter came up to me and said, "Hey, Kelly, can I talk to you?"

I said, "Sure, let's talk." We went into a dressing room, and he asked if he could ask me some questions because he heard that I was losing my vision. I told him my story. It came out in the Halifax paper before Christmas. He worked for the *Chronicle-Herald*, the big newspaper in Halifax. Back then, playing junior hockey in Nova Scotia, all the local reporters were at the rink doing stories.

It got picked up by a wire service and it went right across Canada. My relatives out west didn't know about my vision yet. Once the story broke, other people started coming around the rink and asking me questions.

The end of my last season playing junior was bittersweet. The team made it all the way to the Centennial Cup, and I had made it back from my injury in time for the playoffs. I was the guy that would go in front of the net and hack and whack and look for loose pucks. I scored a few goals in Winnipeg in the Cup, and we won a few games at the start of the tournament. And then we lost in the semifinals.

Once the season ended, I had a decision to make. Was I going to continue to play competitive hockey, or was I going to focus on school? At that time, Rob Forbes was a player/coach with Bridgewater in the Nova Scotia Senior Hockey League. Bridgewater drafted me, knowing that I was visually impaired. I chose not to play. The team practiced in Halifax, but their games were in Bridgewater, an hour away. I chose school over playing senior hockey.

My fourth year of university was all about school. I played some intramural hockey, but school was the focus. It was my best year academically. With my improved marks, if I did well on my LSAT, the Law School Admission Test, I could get into law school. I wrote the LSAT and also applied to the two-year education program at Saint Mary's to become a teacher.

I received a letter telling me that I was accepted into the Saint Mary's education program. Soon afterwards, I received a phone call from Dalhousie University. They told me they had a spot open in their law school. They wanted to know if I was interested in being interviewed. This was what I really wanted. I went and did the interview and one week later I got a call telling me that I was accepted into law school at Dalhousie. I was happy.

I received the necessary accommodations I requested during my time at law school without issue.

I have requested accommodation in my new role as a Judge and I am still waiting for those accommodations to be implemented. My colleagues ground me and support me, telling me that I am entitled to these accommodations.

Requesting accommodations, I find personally challenging, because I do not want to be seen as less than anyone else because of my vision impairment.

Notwithstanding my vision impairment, I wanted to do everything exactly as everyone else was doing. I was determined to graduate with my classmates at the same time that they did. It wasn't easy, but I did it. People kept asking me and telling me that I was entitled to these accommodations. But I never wanted to be seen as less than anyone else. Even if I had a vision impairment, I wanted to do every-thing exactly as everyone else was doing. I was determined to gradu-ate with my classmates at the same time that they did. It wasn't easy, but I did it. Back then, they had these devices to help me read, and it would take me longer to read a textbook then everyone else. Now, with smartphones and more modern technology, reading for me is a lot easier.

The first ten years of my law career, I almost exclusively did crimi-nal defence work. I loved working in the courtroom, and for a long time nobody knew about my vision problems. I came up with ways to keep that private.

Police officers have handwritten notes, and they also have some-thing called a Crown sheet: a narrative that is supposed to reflect the officer's notes. There were times there were discrepancies between the two. I would have my assistant type it all up and I would read it before we went into court so I knew exactly what was in the officer's notes. In court, I would stand and hold the notes a few feet away from my face for dramatic effect. I couldn't see them, but I knew what they said.

Over time, people learned about my vision and got wise to my court-room tricks. Even now, though, at times I keep my vision problems to myself. I am not sure why. Perhaps it's just habit. I suppose I don't want people to look at me differently, and I don't want to be excluded. But mostly, I just don't want to get into the story and have to explain that I can't see certain things. Most times when people see me struggling with my vision, they'll say, "Oh, you should put your glasses on." Like that is going to help! Often, I will fib and say, "Oh, I forgot my glasses, can you tell me what that says?"

In summer 2015, I got a phone call from a guy named Peter Par-sons who was also visually impaired. By this time, I had talked to the kids at the Halifax School for the Blind. I had done some work for the

CNIB, and I had met a kid who had the same eye disease as me. Peter introduced me to the kid and asked if I would talk to him and see if I could help. I was just trying to give back and help them by sharing my experiences. Peter had heard about blind hockey, and I was surprised he hadn't told me about it earlier, because Peter is into blind sports.

He asked me if I'd mind sharing my contact information with a guy named Matt Morrow, with Canadian Blind Hockey. I was confused. *What is Canadian Blind Hockey?* But I agreed. Later, Matt reached out to me and said, "If you are ever interested in learning about blind hockey, we can talk."

Back then, I was travelling a lot as an adjudicator for residential school claims. I was going to be in Vancouver, where Matt lives, two weeks after talking to him. We met in August, and he told me all about blind hockey, which is the same as regular example with the exception of the puck. Blind hockey uses a larger, adapted puck that makes noise as it moves around the ice.

He said I would be great for blind hockey, and I was thinking, *You haven't even seen me on the ice. How do you know I would be good?* I was intrigued, though, about the rules and the special puck, and everything else. In blind hockey, players with the most vision play forward. Players with less vision play defence and goalie. In most cases, goalies have very little vision or are completely blind.

In March 2016, they were putting on a tournament in Toronto and invited me. I showed up at the Mattamy Athletic Centre (formerly Maple Leaf Gardens), having no clue what to expect. I walked into the dressing room, and it was your typical hockey scene, only there were white canes and some guide dogs. There were also people like me, holding their phone close to their face. I felt right at home!

Out on the ice, I watched some of the practice. There was a mix of younger kids and older players, and a wide variety of skill levels. Some players could really skate while others were still working on their basic skills.

They split us up into four teams, and I joined one that was coached by Paul Cairns. Paul was best friends with Mark DeMontis, who is heavily involved in blind hockey. Paul went around the room and asked everyone about what level of hockey they had played and what their level of vision was like.

It was neat hearing everyone else's stories. There were two younger guys who said they had Stargardt disease. I was shocked; I had hardly met anyone else who had the same condition as me. I was forty-six years old at this point. It was awesome to know that I wasn't alone.

The younger guys started asking me about these new features and apps on their phone. I didn't have a clue what they were talking about. They had their phones set up so they would read to them. I didn't know you could do that. I was more interested in talking to the other guys about their challenges of living life as a visually impaired person. The hockey was secondary.

When we got on the ice, I quickly realized how important it was to know your teammates and how well they could see. I had the puck in the offensive zone, and I was always taught to share the puck. I came out from behind the net, and I looked towards the point, and my teammate François Beauregard was banging his stick. I passed the puck, and it stopped a foot in front of him. It stayed there. François didn't play the puck.

I was so confused. I started yelling at him to get the puck. A player on the other team came by, grabbed the puck, and skated down the ice. I talked to François afterwards and realized the issue. My central vision is full of dots and spots, and everything is blurry. However, my peripheral vision is fairly intact. I know when the puck is on my stick, and I can handle it. François said his vision is like looking through a straw. He could have seen it if I had yelled to him. I was keeping my mouth shut, thinking he saw me, and I didn't want the other team to know. In blind hockey, you *really* have to communicate, and you have to know what your teammate's vision is like.

I joined blind hockey at the perfect time. They had a lot of players who loved playing and they were improving their hockey skills. The program took off and we were able to identify other players from out west.

We picked up two guys in their twenties who had played Junior B hockey in Alberta. They both had Stargardt's like me. We had great coaches, and they were excellent at taking your typical high-intensity hockey drill and adapting it to the visually impaired.

The sport was growing, and I noticed the compete level in blind hockey never let up. Typically, when you play pickup hockey, nobody backchecks and nobody would get in front of the puck. Usually in pickup hockey, nobody wants to block a shot because they might get hurt.

In blind hockey, it is the complete opposite. Regardless of anyone's ability, everyone is giving their all, game in and game out, and every practice, too.

After the first tournament I played in, I wanted to go to every one I could. I loved the play, but I also wanted to meet and greet other players in the blind hockey community. I ended up going to Chicago, Washington, D.C., and then Pittsburgh.

Back in 2019, Russia reached out to Blind Hockey Canada. Their hockey federation paid for everything, and they flew over our program manager. Russia was staging an all-abilities hockey summit. From this, Russia started their first blind hockey program, and it has grown quickly in a few short years. As of now, Russia has at least six kids teams playing blind hockey. They sent us a link to watch one of those games, with announcers calling the game and everything. It was really cool to watch. They were playing with the special pucks that we had sent them.

My ultimate goal was to see as many visually impaired kids as possible start skating and playing hockey. I have two kids, and I coached them when they were younger. They both played Timbits hockey. I remember as a parent how fun it was on the road. The kids would be with their friends in the hotel, the parents would have a drink. That was the main driver for me to get involved in blind hockey: I wanted parents of kids who were visually impaired to enjoy the same experiences I had.

Because everything was shut down during the pandemic, we didn't have a program the previous year. But prior to the pandemic, we had our best season ever. We had a training camp in Toronto in August 2019. The Ottawa 67's helped fund our first blind hockey program in the Ottawa area.

After Christmas, we received a note from two guys in Finland who wanted us to come over and host a blind hockey camp.

I was joined by Matt Morrow, Luca DeMontis, and François Beauregard, and we headed to Helsinki at the end of January 2020 to run a blind hockey camp. I ended up running into a teammate of mine, Petri Pusa, who I played junior hockey with when I was in Halifax. Petri had returned to Finland and was now the VP of Bauer sales for the Scandinavian countries. He gave us some sticks for the kids, and he was really nice. The camp in Finland was amazing. We had both females and males, and the camp was held in this excellent training facility located about an hour outside of Helsinki.

One of the players at the camp had come over from Sweden, and he wanted to run a similar program there. We were supposed to go back and do that in Sweden in April 2020, but the pandemic cancelled our plans. We were also in contact with a gentleman from Oxford, England, who wanted to run a summer camp for blind hockey players in August 2020. When everything was shut down in March 2020, all of those plans were scuttled.

To help keep the momentum of blind hockey going through the pandemic, we started doing events online. We don't have a lot of huge sponsors, but the ones that we do have, we wanted them to see we were still relevant.

A sports psychologist that I know did a mental health seminar for our athletes. Rich Clune of the Toronto Marlies is a great guy, and he did a podcast for us. We tried to come up with ways to keep people engaged. We did Zoom meetings and tried to keep everyone involved in blind hockey connected. Without our usual events, we were missing out.

And I wanted to do more than just be involved. I wanted to raise awareness for the sport. That is why I decided to inline skate across Ontario. Mark DeMontis had already skated across Canada. He went from Toronto to Vancouver in 2009. In 2011, he skated from Halifax to Toronto. To be honest, I never knew about those campaigns when they were happening. When I started playing blind hockey, I got to know Mark really well and I learned about his previous efforts.

In May of 2020, during the pandemic, I stepped forward and became the president of the Blind Hockey Association. After, I talked to Mark about the ten-year anniversary of his last skate from Halifax to Toronto. I asked him about what part of Canada he had not skated through. We thought about skating through Newfoundland, but after looking into it we decided the logistics didn't work. We decided to skate from Windsor to Ottawa in ten days and try to raise $100,000.

Once we came up with a plan, I was all in.

The challenge was to come up with a route and do it as safely as possible. We originally thought we would have four inline skaters and would do 25 kilometres a day. Then we thought we should do something that was safer. We decided to skate 100 kilometres a day and spread it out across Ontario. We felt it was safer to avoid busier roads. There was less of a chance of something going wrong.

We started it at Assumption Park at the Ambassador Bridge in Windsor. We skated the waterfront trail and different parts of the city, through parks and other safer areas. We didn't feel comfortable skating along the 401 highway. We did some of it on roads and highways, but not too much.

We had this big RV as our rolling home base. The RV had decals of all of our sponsors on it and stuff like that. We took a few people by surprise with our setup. They'd ask, "What in the heck? Blind hockey?" Then they would ask us what we were doing, and when we told them they dug deep into their pockets and donated money. We had a plastic Stanley Cup that we used to collect donations. We had this postcard made up that we gave out to people along the way. It had the #Courage21 hashtag on the front, and on the back, it had a list of all the stops we were making with a QR code for people to donate. We called it #Courage21 because we wanted to do something coming out of Covid. It was something to get people fired up and programs back up and running. Just before Covid, I was part of Canadian Blind Hockey and we had gone over to Finland and put on a hockey camp. Things were going well, and other countries were interested and then Covid shut everything down. When I took over as the president of Canadian Blind Hockey, our goal was to restart all of our programs.

Programs need money and raising some was important; raising awareness for blind hockey was even more important. Every time someone chooses to tell my story, people learn about blind hockey, and that is a win in itself. After I took over, I wanted to maintain a presence in the blind community as we exited Covid, and we needed funding to reopen our programs in 2021. With the #Courage21 campaign, we were able to raise $100,000. We worked hard to raise that money, and we had some good corporate sponsors who stepped up and helped us. A lot of friends and family and other people who wanted to donate to the cause all made a big difference.

Every time along our journey we were able to engage someone, they would tell us, "I never knew about blind hockey." Every time was a success because we were getting the word out. The media coverage we received helped, and people got the word out on social media. I know there are parents out there with a child who is partially sighted, or even legally blind. These parents won't put their kids in hockey, and they don't believe it is even an option for them. I want to tell all of them, their vision problems don't have to keep them out of the game. We received a lot of admiration along the way and a lot of heartfelt encouragement. That meant a lot.

Hockey Canada has been really good to us, and we are in the first stage of becoming an official partner with Hockey Canada. They have a three-stage process, and we are past the first stage. While that is going on, Hockey Canada is sharing training materials with us to help us grow the program. I hope that in the future, we can become full partners with Hockey Canada.

We continue to write proposals for grants and funding. We were able to secure a sizeable grant from Sport Canada to host multi-discipline camps in the summer. Not just a hockey camp, but other blind sports as well. The first multi-sport summer camp for blind athletes was held at Saint Mary's University. It went well; the only complaint that we heard was that everyone was staying in dorm-style rooms without air-conditioning. Other than that, it was a good camp, and Saint Mary's coaching staff and the athletic admin team was amazing and treated us like pros. We basically had full run of the campus for the entire week and the kids loved it.

Everyone should have a chance to experience and play at whatever level they are happy with.

I want kids that join blind hockey to have something to aspire to. I want them to think that they can play for Team Canada someday and wear the maple leaf on their chest. Exposure to the national program is important. It gives kids something to work towards.

When I became a lawyer, my goal was to stick up for the underdog. I wanted to help the person that didn't have the ability to stand up for themselves. It's part of the reason I adjudicated Indian residential school claims all across Canada. My mom is English and Métis. My aunt had gone to a residential school. At first, I hadn't heard much about it, other than what I had read in the media. In my view, it was going to be the biggest settlement of wrongs perpetrated on Indigenous people in Canada. The work that needed to be done and still needs to be done to reconcile these past wrongs and move forward is immense. I wanted to be a part of it.

That work took me right across Canada, to many different communities, hearing so many heartbreaking stories. Some of these communities had very high expenses and few resources, and it made me appreciate all the luxuries and conveniences I grew up with all the more. Those experiences pushed me to make life a little better for people, however I could.

Canadian Blind Hockey's goal is to grow the sport within Canda and internationally. Collectively our ultimate dream is to have blind hockey included in the Paralympics.

The NHL is now starting to partner with Canadian Blind Hockey. During the 2024 NHL All-Star weekend in Toronto, the league gave Canadian Blind Hockey a booth at the fan expo. They brought in a net, blind hockey pucks, and other things so fans at the expo could experience what blind hockey is all about. Ideally, we would be able to demo blind hockey at the Winter Paralympics in Italy 2026.

For the time being, I am a happy man. I have my beautiful,

supportive wife, Patricia. I have my family and I have my hockey. After spending some time in Ottawa, I moved back home to Halifax in summer 2020. Upon my return I practiced law, and that year I was fortunate to be a player mentor/advisor with the Saint Mary's University Huskies hockey team. I went on the ice with the team once a week, and the level of play was impressive.

In June 2022 I was appointed as a judge for the Provincial Court of Nova Scotia. In Ontario they call it the Ontario Court of Justice now. That is the same level of court that I preside over in Nova Scotia. Some provinces refer to their provincial court by different names. No matter what they call it, my role as a judge, presiding over a trial, is no different.

Prior to my judicial appointment, I was doing some work with Hockey Nova Scotia as a part of their diversity and inclusion committee. There isn't one person at Hockey Nova Scotia that I have talked with that hasn't been wonderful in helping me grow the sport of blind hockey. In June of 2024, I was beyond thrilled to see Mark DeMontis win the NHL's Willie O'Ree Community Hero Award. That was a big moment for the Canadian Blind Hockey Association.

Great organizations like these make such a difference. I am here to tell you that no matter what, "vision or no vision," you can still play hockey and love it as much as I do. To this day, I still play sighted hockey, as well as blind hockey. When we work together, there's a space for everyone to play hockey.

https://canadianblindhockey.com/

8

The Community Builder

Rob Kerr

I was never an elite player and I never played on a travel team. Still, I owe everything I have to the game of hockey.

I learned good lessons from being around the game. I had good mentors along the way, guys like John Short and Peter Maher. A respected journalist, Short is a member of the Alberta Sports Hall of Fame. The longtime voice of the Calgary Flames, Peter Maher is a hockey broadcasting legend. I have been around some really good people, and seeing what they did, I felt that is how you are supposed to be. You are supposed to give back in any way that you can.

There is a group of us here in Calgary who have worked on a bunch of projects in the last decade or so. I sit on boards and like to be involved that way, but I prefer to roll up my sleeves and do events. In April of 2024, after ten years, I stepped down as a director for Sport Calgary. I stepped down from the Flames Kids Sports board to allow another member to join the board. Having said that, I still do some work for the Kids Sports board.

More gets done. When it comes to charity, we need to be more proactive: that's the role I see for sports teams moving forward.

I advocate on behalf of the non-elite player. The people I work with in my circle are the same way. We are passionate about making sure the game is accessible and available to all.

My first and best mentors were my parents. Growing up in Alberta, hockey is what my dad and I bonded over. We were a big hockey family. But my dad got sick in 1974: he was diagnosed with Crohn's disease. I was four years old. He was relatively healthy before the diagnosis. At the time, it was devastating news. Now it is something you treat with pills and live a fairly normal life, but not back then in the seventies.

I am six feet three inches tall, and I weigh over two hundred pounds. My dad has the same frame as me, but when he was really ill in 1976, he weighed less than a hundred pounds. They had pictures of him in medical textbooks.

My mom is a fighter, and she wouldn't let him die. She found a doctor at the University of Alberta who took my dad on as a patient. This doctor put my dad on a new therapy based on the steroid cortisone. It is commonplace now, but at the time it wasn't at all. That doctor kept my dad alive.

My dad had a lot of reasons not to do things in life, justifications for quitting, but he never did. He ran his own business and sometimes would work seven days a week. He did all this even though he had a colostomy bag, and he was fed with an IV when he got home. This is in the late 1970s, and my dad was fed by that IV at home for almost a year. I grew up watching this man who fought like hell to live, but he also wouldn't be defined by his illness.

My mom was his primary caregiver, and she sat on the board of what was then called the Canadian Foundation of Ileitis and Colitis. Despite everything going on in her life and all of her struggles, I saw my mom giving back. To be honest, I didn't start to do charity work until later. I was in my late thirties when I really got involved. In my youth it was all about hockey.

I missed getting my high school diploma by one credit. But I do have a forest technology diploma. My job in the early nineties was working as a forest officer in Fort McMurray for the Alberta Forest Service. I met my wife, Frankie, in Fort McMurray. She was also a forest officer, and she still is to this day. This was back in 1992, when the Alberta Winter Games were coming to our town.

We were getting married that fall and she was intent on volunteering. She talked about it a lot, and it started bothering me because I wasn't keen to. Finally, I went down to the volunteer office, which was in an old video store. I went in on my lunch break and they asked me, "What can we do for you?"

I looked at them and said, "I am here to volunteer." To be honest, my goal was to show up my wife.

They asked me, "Well, what do want to do?"

All the jobs that they needed were written on a big board. My eyes found the words "Play-by-play hockey." I pointed and said, "I'll do that!" I had never done anything like that before. I thought if I was going to volunteer, I might as well do something I like.

I lived in Edmonton during the Stanley Cup years of the eighties. Because of the power of AM radio, I knew all about the Oilers and the Flames and their announcer, Peter Maher. As a kid, I would take a small radio into bed and listen to different stations. When I would visit relatives in Calgary, I could search the radio at night and pick up radio stations from the United States. I could easily listen to KMOX from St. Louis.

I loved listening to the storytellers on the radio. Before the internet, we didn't have all kinds of information at our fingertips. I can still remember my excitement hearing the voice of the Oilers, Rod Phillips, lose his mind about a big goal from Wayne Gretzky. The announcers were gods to me. So even though I had zero experience, when I saw "play-by-play" on that board, I knew I had to try it.

The volunteer office put me in touch with the local cable company and TV station in Fort McMurray who were in charge of producing everything. They said they had someone to do hockey but asked me if I would take a camera and go out and do stories. Sure, why wouldn't I?

So, throughout the Winter Games I would pull people aside and ask them about their experiences there, what the games meant to them, and all kinds of things. I didn't get to do interviews until towards the end of the event. And I didn't have the wardrobe for it. I had an ill-fitting suit, and that was it. We were so overwhelmed trying to do everything and cover everything, we were doing voiceovers for stories, sitting in a van outside venues. The first one that I did, I did it in one take. I didn't think anything of it at the time. It was only later in life that I realized that is a skill that is essential for a broadcaster.

It was community cable in 1992 and a free-for-all. We were making it up as we went.

After the games were over, the local community cable station asked me if I could help them with the production of the Fort McMurray Oil Barons games. I was the happiest guy in the world. My new gig was Camera 3, the follow cam. I learned how to run cable and set up a camera, but more than that, I was part of something.

One day, the guy doing play-by-play didn't show up for a playoff game. I jumped in and did my first game. I had no time to talk to anyone, I just did it. I was set to operate Camera 3 and kept hearing through my headphones that the person who was supposed to call the game was nowhere to be found. The producer then asked me if I thought I could do it, and I said sure.

I wasn't very good at it, but I loved it.

I started volunteering calling the Oil Barons games when they asked me what I would like to do. I told them, "What I really want to do is a late-night talk show." All of sudden, I ended up doing a Tuesday evening talk show in Fort McMurray called *Northern Prime*. The show was sixty minutes long, and I did almost everything. My wife would book the guests, and between the two of us, we would write out the cue cards the night before. But other than that, it was all me. I had no idea what I was doing, so I just did it.

We never had any real special guests on, but we had the mayor on, that was fun. We had members of the Fort McMurray Oil Barons on. Chris Phillips, the former longtime member of the Ottawa Senators, was with the Oil Barons at the time as a sixteen-year-old. We talked about him all the time, but we never had him on. Because it was such an off-the-cuff show, probably the biggest guest we ever had was the guests we created. We created something called "Raven Man," which was Fort McMurray's only superhero. It was one of the camera operators dressed up in a costume and he became a reoccurring guest. He was our version of Larry "Bud" Melman from the David Letterman show.

Between the talk show and calling Oil Barons games, for the next three years I put in thirty to forty hours a week, on top of my job as a forest officer. I was happy doing it and didn't think anything would change. Then fate intervened.

In 1995, Alberta premier Ralph Klein decided he didn't need civil servants, so the government started offering buyouts. My wife and I both took one for our forestry jobs. I was twenty-five years old. I applied to SAIT, the Southern Alberta Institute of Technology, to enter a radio and TV program.

When I was accepted, we moved to Calgary, and I went to school. My wife took a buyout from the government and started working for a private contractor, still working in the forest industry. There is no question that my wife, Frankie, was the breadwinner in the family at the time.

Before classes began, they had a sign-up to join various clubs, and the hockey coach was there. I started talking to him about the Oil Barons and various players in the Alberta Junior Hockey League. Ken invited me to a practice with his SAIT Trojans hockey team and said, "I could use some help."

I was an average player, and an older student, and I wasn't sure what I should do. I talked to my dad later that night. He told me, "Rob, that's how you get experience and build your résumé." I went back the next day and started working for the coach, Ken Babey. Right away, I had an immediate respect for Ken. I listened and learned from him every chance that I could get. Ken was connected to Hockey Canada, and he was connected to other countries. He was a big influence to me when it came to connecting community to sports. Even in the mid-nineties, Ken was way ahead when it came to having athletes involved in the community and teaching them responsibility.

He had no assistants, so I chased pucks and helped any way I could and learned the game inside and out. The next year, Ken became the athletic director at SAIT, and he hired me because they needed somebody to do media. I was in my second year of my program and working for the Athletic Department. It went well and pretty soon it was successful. I never finished my program at SAIT.

One year later one of my instructors at school called me up, "Hey, Estevan is looking for a news guy and someone who can do play-by-play in the SJHL," the Saskatchewan Junior Hockey League. I had to look at a map to find where Estevan was. I was shocked to see it was the eastern side of Saskatchewan. I was really hoping it was on the western side of the province.

I sent the radio station in Estevan a tape of my play-by-play with the Fort McMurray Oil Barons. They flew my wife and me out to Estevan and offered us jobs. I was going to do afternoon news at CJ 1280 AM in Estevan, and then I would call the Estevan Bruins games in the fall. We bought a house in Estevan, *before* I officially had the job. It cost us $48,000. I loved Estevan. I started at the radio station, doing afternoon news. And then I called the games for the Estevan Bruins of the SJHL. Life is different in a small town in the prairies. A few months after we had moved to Estevan, a couple asked my wife and me if we wanted to join them for dinner. They suggested that we go to Red Lobster. I was confused because there wasn't a Red Lobster in Estevan. They meant in Regina, and so they thought nothing of driving two hours to Regina to have dinner at Red Lobster, and then drive two hours to come home. That was the kind of thing you did in Estevan. For a small town like Estevan, the Bruins were on the cutting edge at the time when it came to broadcasting games on the internet and giving people a chance to listen to games, no matter where they lived.

I started doing marketing for the team and media relations, while continuing to call their games for radio.

After a year of working in Estevan, the Bruins decided they wanted some help. I had paid my way to attend a sports marketing conference in Anaheim that first year in Estevan, which would now come in handy. During the 1999–2000 season, I found out about this sports business conference being held in Anaheim. I talked to my parents about it, and they told me that I should go and check it out. I arrived from Estevan, representing the Bruins, and they had executives from the Kansas City Royals and the Miami Dolphins and all of these major league teams. I went to the various breakout sessions during the conference, and Cary Kaplan, the president of the Hamilton Bulldogs, an AHL team at the time, was there. During one of the sessions we met another couple that was Canadian and had lunch. We hit it off right away. They had a mixer later on. Cary convinced me to attend because he had some people he wanted to introduce me to.

Cary introduced me to the person who was running the Louisville Panthers, the AHL farm team for the Florida Panthers. I guess he enjoyed our conversation because two weeks later, the guy I met from Louisville said to me, "How quickly can you get down to Minot, North Dakota? We want to fly you and your wife to Louisville, and we want to offer you a job."

The lawyers for the Louisville Panthers had completed all of my paperwork and documentation and then they called to prep me. They said that when I drive to the border, ask for a work visa. Then the border agents would talk to me for five minutes, then they would spend twenty minutes doing a background check. They said it would take around thirty minutes, and then I could be on my way to Louisville.

I decided to drive to the border, get my visa, go back and get my wife and our stuff and then drive to Louisville. I got to the border and told them I was looking for a work visa. Well, four hours later, I was rejected by the United States. For some reason, the team lawyer never asked me about my education. When I got to the border, that was the first thing they asked me about. When they discovered that I had nothing but a forest technology diploma, they quickly said no.

This was one year before 9/11, when travel and work permits were relatively simple. But for whatever reason, they didn't view me as a viable visa candidate. We drove back to my mom's house in Edmonton. For close to a year, I was collecting employment insurance. It was the only time in my life that I collected EI from the government. I was humbled by the whole thing, and slightly embarrassed. While I collected EI, I was volunteering for various organizations.

Not long after, I was sitting at my mom's home, all of our stuff in storage in Estevan. I heard John Short on the radio. I grew up listening to him and I was a big fan. I sent John an email (still a new thing at that time). I let him know that I was a big fan. I was surprised when he replied. He said, "Hey, we do a show at Northlands racetrack. If you ever want to come up and watch, stop by."

I had nothing else to do, so I took him up on the offer. Two weeks later, I was hosting my first-ever sports talk show, working with John. We started an internet company, doing play-by-play for AJHL and high school hockey. We were ten or fifteen years ahead of current trends. At that time, we couldn't monetize the internet, though.

A while later, John moved on to CJCA radio, the Christian station. He decided to put on a sports talk show there, too. They asked me if I wanted my own show. Of course I did! My show was called *Just a Game, with Rob Kerr*. The show ran weeknights from 11 p.m. to 1 a.m.

It's not so easy to set up a new show, though. I took a $50,000 loan from the bank to buy my own airtime. Then we sold our own ads to cover our costs. It was fantastic and we even got the odd phone call in to the show, which wasn't bad for a little sports show.

I did that for a year, when the job to be the Flames' radio host became available. At first, I didn't want it because it would mean leaving my mom home alone in Edmonton. My dad had passed away in September of 1998. When my mom found out what I was thinking, she told me, "I will move to Calgary." I got the job in May 2003.

When I got the job in Calgary, I felt that I had finally arrived. This was after the failed Team Radio experience. 960 AM in Calgary was part of that. Even though the Team concept failed, 960 AM kept the sports format. When I arrived in Calgary in May, I worked all these extra shifts on the station, including on the morning show for a month. I would have guests and call people and talk sports. When the hockey season started, at the beginning of the 2003–2004 season, I hosted a one-hour show called *The Hockey Show*. Peter Maher, the voice of the Flames, was a guest on every show, and so I would have other guests on to fill out the time. After the Flames game was over, I would do a post-game show and just kept going and taking calls. I was so happy to come to Calgary and I arrived at the perfect time. After not making the playoffs for years, the Flames went all the way to the Stanley Cup Final that season. The city of Calgary will never forget that playoff run; it was magical. I would stretch my post-game show for over six hours some nights. I never understood the concept of the producer getting paid overtime because I was making him work so late. Fans were calling in and I wanted them to get on the air and talk about the Flames. We were creating an audience and making them a part of the show.

That year, the city turned into the "Red Mile." I did eight years of radio, three years of TV, then was back on the radio for four more years. My radio show ran weekdays from 3 to 6 p.m., then it got moved to 2 to 6 p.m. I was also hosting some remotes on the weekend, especially when the Flames went on that deep playoff run.

It was during this time in Calgary that I started to become more active in giving back and using my platforms to try to make things better. I got to know Bob Nicholson in those days, when he was with Hockey Canada (which is based in Calgary). The folks at Hockey Canada were always good to me, and I would attend World Junior camps at Father David Bauer Arena. Around 2006, I interviewed Bob and he mentioned that there was an arena shortage in Calgary. In 1967, there had been a big build going in Canada when all these arenas went up. By the 2000s, a lot of those arenas were beginning to fall apart, and nobody was building new ones. Bob mentioned that Calgary needed at least fifteen more ice sheets to satisfy the demand.

I went to my boss with Sportsnet 960 and said I wanted to do something, to talk about the arena shortage in Calgary. I loved doing my afternoon show remotely and I would go all over Calgary. We did the next show live from the Max Bell Arena, and we talked all afternoon about the arena shortage in the Calgary area. This is the same Max Bell Arena that hosted curling and short-track speed skating at the 1988 Winter Olympics.

We did a few more shows about the issue and were able to build some momentum and plant the seed that we needed more arenas in Calgary. I would make sure to book a guest from KidSport and talk about their charity, and the difficulties kids were having getting access to ice. I did weekend shows for Sportsnet 960, for Hockey Calgary and Hockey Canada, too, talking about getting more new Canadians and more girls involved in hockey. This was in addition to my afternoon show I hosted on weekdays.

When people ask me why it is so important to get more girls

involved in hockey, I tell them because there is no reason not to. When I had the opportunity to do things, I noticed this hashtag on social media, #HockeyIsForEveryone. I had the pleasure of working with Cassie Campbell-Pascall when she was an analyst on Flames hockey. During road games, we would sit together at Schanks sports bar and talk hockey. As a kid, I knew about women's hockey teams. I came from a progressive family. In the eighties and the early nineties, my wife was a forest officer and I heard all of the nonsense that she had to deal with. Without knowing it, I was learning about DEI, diversity, equity, and inclusion, three decades before anybody invented the term. I was living it in my family and the people that I was around. There is no reason to use gender as a reason to tell someone they can't do something, that makes no sense. I want my kids to have the same opportunities everyone else has. Take a look at the Professional Women's Hockey League and how popular it has become. It is great, but it is somewhat embarrassing that it took this long to get here.

In 2011, I read a story in the *New York Times* about the local reporters who covered City Hall in New York. Every Christmas they would put on a pageant and a luncheon for underprivileged kids. I thought it would be cool if we could do something similar in Calgary. Even though other reporters worked for competing broadcast companies, we all got along.

I began speaking with my fellow media members about how not every kid gets to go to a hockey school. Hockey was becoming an elite game and moving further out of reach for a lot of people. The cost of equipment and training, ice availability, and travel were all contributing factors. We all pitched in and held our own hockey camp for kids. In 2012, we launched the Control-F camp, for kids who had never gone to a hockey camp before. Control-F was all about Calgary, teamwork, respect, leadership, and fun. It was all volunteers from the sports media community in Calgary. Those hallmarks were always big for me. I am big believer in teamwork. Google had just come out and all these domain names were popping up. We just called it CTRL-F and the name stuck.

Kevin Hodgson, who won the Willie O'Ree Award in 2021, was a big help. He runs a program called HEROS (Hockey Education Reaching Out Society).

Al Coates, the Calgary Flames GM, and Kevin Webster from Kid-Sport Calgary were a big help as well. Al Coates also brought me on to the Sports Bank board. In Edmonton, there is a long-running organization that takes used hockey equipment and other sports equipment, cleans it up, and gives it to kids so they can play sports. It had been around for close to three decades in Edmonton, but there was nothing similar in Calgary. Bill Comrie, the founder of The Brick Furniture shops, couldn't understand why Edmonton had something like this and Calgary didn't. He wrote a check for a total of $500,000 spread over five years. At the beginning, it was called the Comrie Sports Equipment Bank. Once we got up and running, we aligned with Kid-Sport, and the Flames Foundation jumped on board as well. In 2018 I started working for the Calgary Hitmen of the WHL and the pro lacrosse team, the NLL Calgary Roughnecks.

In 2018, I retired from broadcasting and went to work for the Calgary Hitmen, and the team was approached by a representative from the province who was doing some work with the Siksika Nation and Siksika Health. The Indigenous nation is located about an hour east of Calgary. They wanted the Hitmen to do a practice out there and provide some tickets for the community. I am a big believer that the community has a big role to play in sports, both professional and amateur. At the Hitmen games, we did a lot of the typical junior hockey events like the Teddy Bear toss. I told them that I could set that up, but it didn't seem to be enough. I asked them, "Can we talk about doing something more?"

We set up a meeting and went out to meet with Siksika Health CEO Dr. Tyler White. Dr. White is instrumental in my work with First Nations. They have an opioid issue, like many communities have. But they are also forward thinking: they believe that sport and recreation have a role to play in health.

In January 2019, the Hitmen came out to Siksika Nation for a full practice. We had a big day planned. They wanted to know exactly when we would arrive because they wanted to introduce the team to the elders and the band council. They also wanted a complete list of names of everyone who was going to be there. When we arrived, all the players and coaches and management were brought in to meet the band council and an elder who did a prayer. When the prayer ended, they did a smudging ceremony. It is tradition that when they do this ceremony, you give tobacco. We came ready with a pouch.

At the end of the explanation of the smudging the elder looked at the players and said, "I don't know what your beliefs are, but if you would like to come up and participate, please do. But don't feel that you have to. We know you have to go on the ice and practice." Every single one of our players went up and participated in the smudging ceremony. This is the beauty of having communities involved in sports. It's not just us giving back. Everyone benefits. Our players were being exposed to the Blackfoot culture.

After that, players got their equipment on and prepared for what they thought would just be another practice. We hit the ice and they were playing music in the arena; it was like a rock 'n' roll practice, with fans there. Former Flames great Joel Otto was our assistant coach at the time and the fans went nuts for him.

The Siksika leaders and Dr. White asked us if after practice they could take us over to the gym for a quick meal and, if it was okay, we could sign some autographs. When we walked in, every player, coach, and trainer—and even the bus driver—had a nameplate ready at their seat. We signed autographs nonstop for an hour. The kids coming through to get autographs could not have been nicer. Then they served us dinner and afterwards put on a traditional dance ceremony. We ended it off with a round dance. Round dancing is a longtime First Nations ritual that dates back centuries. The gym was packed with everyone holding hands as we danced in a circle. It was an incredible experience. This was not your typical junior hockey public appearance, and the players couldn't stop talking about it after. We were so moved, we decided to do something more.

On February 1, 2020, prior to the pandemic, we held a game to honour the Siksika and the Blackfoot Nations. We wanted to do something beyond a ceremonial puck drop. Siksika purchased 3,500 tickets for Indigenous youth in the Treaty 7 lands in Alberta. We built the whole game-day program around their anthem and their songs, intertwined with our songs and usual game-day rituals.

One of our former players who is Indigenous, Brent Dodginghorse, dropped the puck before the game. During the second intermission, we did a traditional Blackfoot round dance. We did the round dance across the entire concourse of the Saddledome. We had all the fans come out to the concourse at the Saddledome and looped everyone around the entire arena. It wasn't officially the world's largest. We just called it that because the round dance went completely around the concourse. We thought it sounded more big-time if we called it the "world's largest." Even it wasn't the biggest, it was still a sight to see so many people taking part in something with so much meaning to the First Nations people.

We also wanted to do something for people who couldn't come to the game, so they could feel like they were a part of it. We asked if we could do the game in Blackfoot as well as English. Sportsnet had already done a TV game in Cree.

There is an Indigenous radio station that broadcasts throughout Alberta, and they came on board. Siksika provided the broadcast crew, and they broadcast the game in Blackfoot. In the third period, we were able to clip some of their highlights and play them over the jumbotron in the arena. That was really cool. For us, it set the new standard for how to do those kinds of games. Even better, we won the game, beating the Red Deer Rebels. Then the Blackfoot drummers came on the ice and performed the Siksika victory song.

The following Wednesday, Siksika Health came to the Saddledome and trained our players and coaches and HEROS hockey All-Star kids who were high school aged, and one of the groups we were working with on administering naloxone, the rapid treatment for an opioid overdose, like an EpiPen for opioids. They spent two hours with us, teaching us how to identify when someone is suffering an overdose, and how to treat them. This training and drug kit truly saves lives. In May, I received a call from Kevin Hodgson. "I have to tell you about this young man, Cody. And do you have another one of the naloxone kits?"

I told him, "I have mine."

"Can I get it from you?"

"Why do you need my kit?"

He told me the story. It was after three in the morning and one of the HEROS kids that were with us during the naloxone training heard a commotion in the alley near his place. He went outside with his mom to see what was happening, and a guy was overdosing on opioids. They gave him the three shots of naloxone from the kit, and it saved his life.

That spring, with the pandemic under way, we talked to the Siksika Nation about writing a proper memorandum of understanding (MOU). I knew what Siksika wanted: to show the world they had a relationship with a sports team that was mutually beneficial. It seems to me Indigenous people as a whole are tired of white people telling them they need help, and then not listening to them. So we went to them and said, "Teach us, help us." An MOU would give us a more formal agreement to continue working together long term, and it would be something both sides could celebrate. The Hitmen are the first Major Junior hockey team to have an MOU with an Indigenous nation. The partnership continues and both sides work in the community. As a consultant now, one of my clients is the Calgary Surge of the Canadian Elite Basketball League. I am working on a similar MOU with the Surge. At the start the mindset was, "wouldn't it be nice if the Calgary Hitmen worked with Siksika First Nation." That turned into, "wasn't it really nice that Siksika worked with the Hitmen." Siksika value the role of mentorship and leadership, but they also value the role of sport and recreation.

Meanwhile the Tsuut'ina Nation, located on the south end of Calgary, rebuilt their sportsplex. They built this incredible arena at the heart of it. And then, by February 2021, we needed to find a new place to play a Covid-shortened season with no fans. The Saddledome was booked with the Calgary Flames and the Stockton Flames and there was no space for the Hitmen anymore. The Tsuut'ina Nation allowed us to play our games out of the Seven Chiefs Sportsplex. What we did in Siksika gave the Tsuut'ina Nation the confidence that they could work with the Hitmen. The Grey Eagle Resort gave us a great deal so we could house our players there and stay in the bubble. This was different than the NHL bubble that was taking place at the same time. We played twenty-three games at the Tsuut'ina facility, and the rink could not have been any better. The Professional Women's Hockey Players Association (PWHPA) came in, and they held some of their Dream Gap Tour games at the Seven Chiefs Sportsplex as well.

In September 2021, we played a preseason game at the Siksika Nation arena. A week later, we played a game at Tsuut'ina. Both of those nights were important for us because they are meaningful partners. I like to think that the Calgary Hitmen are leading the way. Some teams might wear orange shirts, and that's good, but we are going to have an elder talking to our kids, building stronger bonds.

◆　　◆　　◆

Of all the things that I do or am involved with, the SuperHEROS organization is the one that means the most to me. Everything that I have done in my life built to my involvement with the SuperHEROS. It is our biggest success story when it comes to charity work.

Back in 2017, the Pittsburgh Penguins beat the Ottawa Senators in the Eastern Conference Finals. There was a game in that series in which Kyle Turris scored. He didn't talk to the media afterwards and it was a bit of a controversy. What happened was, right after the game, Kyle and his wife went to visit the Capital City Condors, a hockey team for kids with cognitive disabilities.

That fall, I received an email from someone I didn't know. He said, "I need to get a hold of Curtis Lazar." Curtis had been with the Sens, and now he was with the Flames. I didn't work with the Flames, and I didn't know who this person was, so I didn't think much about it. A couple of months later I was doing a remote show on Sportsnet 960 at a sporting goods store and with a half hour to go, I could see this man staring at me. I thought he was a disgruntled fan who wanted to complain about something. As soon as I got off the air, I walked over to him. He said, "Hey, I sent you an email about the Capital City Condors."

His name was Al. We talked for twenty minutes, and he told me a heartbreaking story. His son Evan has autism. Evan had tried to play in house league hockey, but it didn't work out, even though Evan loves hockey and wanted to be a part of a team. I didn't know what I could do or how I could help him.

I called Kevin Hodgson from HEROS, as we have helped each other over the years. Kevin kind of took it over from there. The three of us soon met up and we walked through it. We started meeting with families who had kids with Down syndrome, or autism, or other disabilities. We realized that there was no program for special needs hockey in the West. There was the Special Olympics, but they didn't have hockey, they had floor hockey. Kevin really liked the idea of creating something for them. He went to the board of HEROS with the idea and they said, "Let's try a pilot project."

We called Brian Sutter, because we knew him, and we had done stuff with him in the past. I had barely got the words out of my mouth when Brian said, "We're in." The Sutter Fund gave us $5,000. We also received some money from the Flames Foundation and started the SuperHEROS pilot project. We recruited twenty-four kids, and through Kevin and his work with the HEROS program, we had access to equipment. The NHL Players Association helped us out and so did SportChek. We went to a SportChek location in Calgary with these young boys and girls. It was a challenge. Some kids found the weight of the equipment to be too much, but they got what they needed.

In October 2018, we went on the ice with these young kids at the Max Bell Arena. Most had never skated before, let alone played hockey. But at the end of that first session, most were skating in their own way. Others needed some help. Without question, it was the most incredible thing we had ever seen. But afterwards, I was quite angry. These kids were being kept out of hockey when all they needed was a chance.

From that first day, the SuperHEROS program grew, and it has only gotten better with time. We played a fun exhibition game with the Regina Rebels girls hockey team. The next year, we added a team in Edmonton, a second team in Calgary, and a team in Regina. Now, we have three teams in Calgary, two in Edmonton, one in Regina, one in Winnipeg, and more to come. Even during the pandemic, we had Zoom calls, and NHL players like Matt Dumba and Brenden Dillon would join and talk to the kids.

What we learned in this journey is that the parents of these kids also never felt like they belonged. But hockey is a big community and this program made them feel like a part of it (and they were). Some parents told us that their kid had spent thousands of hours with a speech therapist. But they say that the one hour a week of hockey made a difference in the child's speech. That is why we do the things that we do, stories like that. The more we do it, the more attention we receive and the more support comes our way.

I cannot thank people like Kevin Hodgson enough for all of his efforts. We are at the point now that we have one volunteer for approximately every one and a half kids. It makes such a difference.

There was one kid, Gage. When we first started, two people would have to pick him up and hold him and move him around the ice. Two years later, Gage stands on his own and takes shots. Eventually, he is going to skate around the ice on his own, too. That is what it is all about. Kids like Gage. We have cage trainers now, so we can put kids with cerebral palsy on the ice. The cage trainer is a device that allows someone with a physical disability to stand upright on their skates and, with assistance, move around the ice.

I love volunteering for HEROS and SuperHEROS. They both continue to grow, and I am excited for the future. In March of 2023, we took a SuperHEROS team to Ottawa to play in the Capital City

Condors tournament. That was a milestone for us, and it was very exciting. The players and the parents loved it.

I am also working on something called the 10-20-30 Project. It is a culmination of all of my leadership work over the years. It is a five-module program for boys and girls, targeting the U11 and U16 age groups in hockey.

We want the kids to think ten years from now, how are they giving back to the game of hockey and to the community? We ask them, twenty years from now, how are they giving back to the game? Are they going to be officials or coaches? And finally, thirty years from now, how are you giving back to the sport and to the community where you live?

We are developing the project with Hockey Calgary and have had three teams show interest. We also have had students in the MBA program at the University of Calgary work with us. The students are reviewing the results of players and the parents what their answers to the questions. What we want to do is create a program that can be taken across the country and applied to any sport, not just hockey.

Another one of our goals is to make recreation and sports available to all forty-six First Nations in Alberta. I have a client that I work with called the First Nations Health Consortium. They are brining sports and recreation programs to First Nations communities in Alberta. We have partnered with the NHL to provide NHL Street hockey programming to any First Nations community in Alberta who wants it. We are trying to focus on the more remote communities in Northern Alberta.

The best thing you can get out of hockey is teamwork, leadership, respect, and having fun. When it comes to the elite levels of youth hockey in Canada, there are times I think we have lost our way. There are some who don't feel we should take ice time away from elite players. That is a narrative we have to fix in Canada. It's why I love programs like Super-HEROS so much. Hockey should be for everyone, no matter your ability.

9

The Unlikely Hero

Leonard Lye

I am a civil engineer, but what I do has nothing to do with designing or building. My specialty is statistical hydrology, which is the furthest thing from building stuff you can get. I am an expert in water resources and environmental engineering.

As for my off-time, I don't play hockey at all. I can't even skate.

However, I am the founder and coordinating member of the Tetra Society of Newfoundland and Labrador, a nonprofit organization that tries to find solutions for people with disabilities to help them overcome environmental barriers.

Environmental barriers are many and varied. It also depends on the disability of the individual. Some barriers are easy to fix, and some are quite complicated. Tetra's core focus is to address barriers that affect a person's ability to live life independently due to obstacles in their environment. Environmental barriers include things like steps or curbs that prevent someone with mobility impairment from getting where they need to go. Unfortunately, even with all of our advances, people with mobility impairment continue to face numerous environmental barriers. One of Tetra's founding principles is that people are not marginalized by their disability, but by obstacles in their environment. Tetra works to reduce or eliminate these obstacles. Over more than thirty years, Tetra volunteers have built devices that support communication, eating and drinking, completing household chores and personal care, and mobility.

The coordinator is usually the first point of contact. He or she reviews the request for assistance form from the client or caregiver to see if it fits the mandate of the Tetra Society. A site visit is usually arranged to understand the request better and to see what the client can and cannot do. The project is then assigned to volunteers to work with the client/caregiver/therapist to come up with a solution. The coordinator also helps with fundraising, promotion of the society, recruiting volunteers, and so on.

I started working with them back in 1996. We often made devices to help people play sports or be more active. Over the past twenty-plus years, we have completed over a hundred projects to help people with disabilities.

We get requests all the time for devices, often from the parents or occupational therapists. Usually, we're asked to make some kind of a modification to an existing device to help someone with their daily living. Or it could be something to help enhance recreational activities.

We once made a toileting aid for a very obese man. We made a drinking aid for a child with cerebral palsy. We made numerous walker modifications for clients with different mobility issues. We have designed a motorized piano cart for a music therapist and a platform for wheelchair archery. One time, we converted a wheelchair to all-terrain. We also made a guitar strummer for clients paralyzed on one side and various modified bicycles to accommodate clients with different disabilities.

It was through my work with the Tetra Society that I first learned about Carter Burton and his struggles to play hockey. Carter's occupational therapist contacted me about modifications to a hockey glove. Carter has something called hemiplegic cerebral palsy, which affects his left hand. The fingers curl in such a way that he can't get them into the fingers of a normal hockey glove. He can wear a mitten, but not a normal glove. That was the challenge facing us: how to adapt a hockey glove so Carter could play.

I have never met Carter. He lives in King's Point, which is in central Newfoundland, at least a five-hour drive from where I live. I have lived in St. John's since 1987. I don't even know what he looks like. All I know is that he was eleven years old at the time and he loves to play hockey.

Thanks to his occupational therapist, I was able to ask the necessary questions to design the glove. Our communication consisted of a series of phone calls and emails. The request came during the start of Covid-19, and I wasn't able to go to a store and get a glove until

September 2020. Until then, I'd never handled a hockey glove before. I barely knew what they looked like and certainly didn't know anything about how they were constructed.

At home, I studied the materials and components. I took the gloves apart and saw exactly how they were put together and started to figure out how to adapt one for Carter. Before long I had a plan for what to cut out and what to sew together to make a "mitten" hockey glove for Carter's left hand. It took me a few days of studying to see what to un-stitch, what to cut, and what to stitch up. And it took some experimenting. Hard to believe, but for restitching, I found the best thread to use was dental floss.

Once I found the right needle that would work with the different materials and the "thread," I unstitched the glove, cut out the connecting material for the fingers, and then sewed it back together to create the mitten. When I was done, I put my hand in the glove and it held together and felt comfortable. I was very excited that I had come up with the right plan to make it work.

I sent the glove to Carter, shipping it off with Canada Post. With the Tetra Society, we don't charge for any of our work, so that was the end of it. I don't play hockey, so I didn't think too much of it at the time. To me, it was just another project to help someone with a disability.

I didn't know how much Carter liked the glove until CBC Radio did a story about him and how the glove allowed him to play hockey with his friends. In the story, Carter says to me, "Thank you a lot. Now I have the opportunity to play hockey thanks to you. I just love hockey." That was quite touching. I didn't expect that kind of response, and it was an emotional moment for me. I am just so happy Carter likes the glove!

Soon after the CBC story ran, I received a request from Ottawa. A father reached out to me about his nine-year-old son, and how he has an issue with his right hand. This young man had a similar problem to Carter, only on the opposite hand. In this case, the father sent me the glove to work on. Making the second glove was much easier. I already had the process, and this was a different make of glove than the first one and I found the material better to work with.

The first one was a size 11 junior hockey glove that was purchased at Play It Again Sports, a secondhand store. It wasn't a brand-name glove. Subsequent ones were a larger size and made by well-known hockey companies. The material was softer and easier for the needle to go through.

Once I started work, I was done by the afternoon. When I sent the glove back to Ottawa, the father and his son were incredibly happy.

So far, the requests have only been for modifications to hockey gloves.

I do watch hockey sometimes now. Honestly, I prefer to play pickle-ball and other sports. What I hope is that companies that make hockey gloves will think of a way to make mitten-style gloves. At least if people have the option of using something other than the regular glove, it would be a big help. This way, families won't have to rely on someone like me to make a new glove for them. Modifying the glove wasn't that difficult; that's what makes this a bit sad. I hope this work makes companies at least consider giving people the option. As with many, if not all charities, my hope is that one day our work won't be necessary, that people like Carter will have the option to easily buy the special equipment they need. But until that day, I'll enjoy making it however I can.

To me, what I do isn't anything special. This is what we do at the Tetra Society. Carter's glove is one of many projects that I have worked on. I am just happy that it all worked out and Carter can play hockey with his friends and enjoy the game he loves so much.

I am always happy to work on any Tetra projects. That's the whole purpose of the Tetra Society. We try to eliminate obstacles for people with disabilities.

The feedback has been overwhelmingly positive. The "glove" got the most votes in Canada in the TetraNation competition. I even got a thank-you note from the premier of Newfoundland after the story aired on TV nationwide.

I have made four gloves in total so far. After the story aired on TV, I received a request from a parent in Ottawa. That was the second one, for the right hand. The next two were from Newfoundland. One from Paradise, NL, and the other from Clarenville, NL. This time I added a cuff with an elastic band so that the glove or "mitt" can be tightened and won't fall off.

I guess the "glove" project is special because it sure made a difference to the self-confidence of the kids and allowed them to compete like anyone else. Also, it is easy enough to do and doesn't cost the client a cent. We welcome a donation, but we would not bill anyone.

I just feel lucky to play a small part in helping someone play hockey and enjoy the great game.

10

Haki = Hockey

Jim Paek

Jim Paek and family at the 1985 NHL draft

Everything that I have is because of hockey. I am truly blessed to have played pro for sixteen years and travel the world. There aren't many Korean kids who can say that.

I was born in Seoul, South Korea, in April 1967, and moved to Toronto with my family when I was one year old, in 1968. My father had an opportunity to work at Hospital for Sick Children (SickKids) and he thought it would be a great place to raise a family. My dad wanted to give his family opportunities he never had. I still remember going to work with my dad and getting lemon ice.

I have a brother two years older, and he kind of led the way. When we came to Canada, my parents had no idea about hockey. But being here, you have to, it is part of the lifestyle. By the time I wanted to start playing, my parents were very supportive. One of my earliest hockey memories was getting my first pair of skates at Canadian Tire's bargain bin, tube blades and no ankle support, but I was very thankful.

I wanted to be like my older brother, and everyone in Canada plays hockey, so if I wanted friends I had to play. I also quickly fell in love with the game.

I started playing hockey when I was seven. I joined a house league in Etobicoke, in Toronto, and played my games at the Pine Point Arena. Pine Point wasn't too far from our house. It was a great local rink to start hockey. We won all the games and the championships my first year with Richards Hardware. Pine Point also had a great toboggan hill in the back.

I played Atom and then Minor Novice and loved everything about hockey. By the time I started in Pee Wee, I was playing rep hockey for the Toronto Marlboros. We had a good team and ended up going to the world-famous Quebec Pee Wee tournament. We had a guy on our team named Al Sadowy. He'd matured quickly and looked like a man at only twelve years old. He had the best slap shot I had ever seen. We played the Toronto Flames, who had Ron Tugnutt in net. Al took a shot and dropped Ron like a ton of bricks. His shot was that good, and he was only a kid.

My parents turned into full-fledged Canadian hockey parents, which is good because I was playing in tournaments all over the place. Their idea of a holiday was taking us to Barrie or Quebec or some tournament over the weekend. It's about all we had time for. I was playing Midget hockey with St. Mike's, and from there I went to play for the Oshawa Generals in the OHL.

As supportive as my parents were, we could never ignore our education. I always had to have good grades. Growing up in a Korean home, education was very important, and my siblings were all A students. There are a lot of kids of Korean descent in the Toronto area who are good hockey players. But once you get to a certain level, you have to go to school. I was fortunate my parents allowed me to follow my passion and continue with hockey.

Thank goodness I have an older sister who is a doctor, a brother who is in the pharmacy business, and a little sister who is a lawyer! They were all scholars growing up and so my parents felt okay focusing on their education, which allowed me to play sports. Because since I was a young kid, my goal was to be a hockey player and I didn't think too much about anything else. But my parents made sure that my first pro contract had an education clause.

I joined the Oshawa Generals at the start of the 1984–1985 season. Future NHLer Kirk McLean was one of our goalies. I lived with two different families while playing in Oshawa. My first year I lived with our first-round pick, Shane Whelan, and the next years by myself. The families are truly special people that invite you into their homes and make you part of their families. It was a great way to make a transition to independence, because Mom wasn't there to do everything for you.

The OHL at the time was a rough league, on and off the ice. Toronto is such a multicultural city that I never had any problems with racism as a kid. And the hockey family is pretty good. For the most part, I loved playing for the Generals. However, I heard the odd racial slur during my time in Oshawa.

I remember we were playing the Bulls in Belleville and someone on their team yelled something towards me. Bulls coach Larry Mavety grabbed him and shouted, "Hey!" and it never happened again. I respect Larry for that. The game went on and I scored against their goalie, Craig Billington, and we won the game. (Years later, Biller and I were roommates when we played together with the Ottawa Senators. What a treat that was.)

Other times there wasn't a coach like Larry to straighten the kid out, or maybe no one else heard it, and I would get in a fight to shut the player up. But for the most part, those comments didn't bother me, it was like water off a duck's back. I would look at guys sometimes and say, "Be original, at least." And that could also shut them up. Even if these comments bothered me in the moment, none of those times took me away from my game and what I wanted to be as a hockey player. If you wanted to criticize me, I thought, criticize me on my play.

I was drafted by the Penguins in 1985 and I was invited to training camp. I was surprised that Pittsburgh picked me but blessed to have been drafted. When I look back, I am so glad I got drafted by Pittsburgh. I have great memories and lifelong friends.

The draft was in Toronto that year, so I was fortunate to have my parents there with me. To be honest, I don't remember much. What I remember was I am a Penguin and that they were happy to have me.

When I showed up, I was given a high jersey number. Back then, if you had a high jersey number, you knew you were getting sent back to junior. My airline ticket even had a return date on it. I was determined to make the most of the experience, though, and I learned so much at camp. I was in awe of everything. I remember watching Mario Lemieux take a pair of brand-new skates out of the box and put them on for the first time. He measured a stick, taped it up, and he went out and scored three goals in a training camp game. It was a special time, but it was hard. We practiced twice a day and they really worked us. I also walked around the dressing room and got guys to sign things for me.

After my time in Oshawa, I started my pro career playing for the Muskegon Lumberjacks of the old International Hockey League. Coming from Oshawa with a cozy family feeling to Muskegon felt like I was right out of the movie *Slap Shot*. It was a great introduction to pro hockey. I loved it there because we had great players (legends) and coaches to learn from that gave me a chance to succeed. My years there, we were very successful, and we ended up winning the Turner Cup. The IHL started to expand and get better every year.

After three full years in the minors, I finally made the Penguins. This was at the beginning of the 1990–1991 season.

However, I was ninth on the depth chart for defencemen. Our coach, "Badger Bob" Johnson, wanted me to play and get more ice time. So, he sent me off to play with the Canadian National Team, under Dave King. We played NCAA teams, Canadian university teams, and we played all over Europe.

What an experience that was. That team was full of misfits. We had a bunch of first-round picks on that team and Craig Billington was our goalie. Future NHLers Stu Barnes and Dave Archibald were also on that team. It was a great experience, and it was so different than playing hockey in North America. I had to adapt to the international style of hockey. The majority of international hockey is played on Olympic-sized ice, which is fifteen feet wider than North American–style rinks. There is less hitting, more puck possession, and often a trapping-style defensive system you have to deal with.

Playing for Dave King on the national team really helped my career. I still thank Badger Bob for sending me there, and I'm grateful for all the ice time.

We were in a small town in BC when I got the call from Craig

Patrick, telling me the Penguins were going to call me up for the play-offs. I was like Tom Cruise on *Oprah* jumping up and down on the couch, but I was jumping up and down on the bed. I knew I was going to be a Black Ace, but I was going to the show.

The irony is, I was gone most of the 1990–1991 season, playing for the national team, but in the end, I played more playoff games for the Penguins than I did regular season games that year.

I was still the ninth defencemen on the depth chart, but then in the playoffs, first Paul Coffey got hurt, then Ulf Samuelsson, and finally Peter Taglianetti.

All of sudden, I was thrown into the lineup as a sixth defencemen in our series against the Washington Capitals.

My first game we beat the Capitals 3–1, and Lemieux had a goal and an assist. I was in hockey heaven. In the division finals against Minnesota, Badger Bob put me in the lineup at the beginning of the series. That was amazing enough, but what came next was a dream come true. How many players can say their first NHL goal was in a Cup final game, and assisted by Mario Lemieux? I was on the receiving end of one of the sweetest passes I had ever seen. I was ecstatic for so many reasons. Before I knew it, Mario went and got the puck for me. To top off this incredible night, we won the game, and then I got to raise the Stanley Cup. I was very blessed to be a part of that 1991 Penguins team for that playoff run.

People sometimes ask me, how did I end up in so many photos after we won the Cup? I learned quickly if you wanted to be in a photo, you have to stand beside Mario. I wanted my picture in the newspaper for my parents to see.

Thinking about it now, it seems like yesterday. I am truly honoured that my name, the Paek name, is on the Cup—twice.

The next year, I was with the team the whole season as a depth guy and played nineteen games in the playoffs as we repeated as Stanley Cup champions in 1992.

Along the way I had to learn how to defend guys like Pavel Bure. Oh my gosh, he was fast. And I remember how quick Alexander Mogilny was side to side. I remember Wayne Gretzky and Jari Kurri coming down on me on a two-on-one. You would just give up, and line up at centre ice for the face-off! And defending against Keith Tkachuk was tough; in front of the net, he was like a rock, you couldn't move him.

What really helped me was being able to practice every day with Hall of Famers like Lemieux and Paul Coffey. One day at practice, early in that 1991–1992 season, I wanted to figure out what was up with Coffey's skating. I was skeptical at first that anyone could be *that* good. We did a warm-up drill where we would skate hard from blue line to blue line. I thought, *Let's see what he's all about.* He took two strides, and he was already at the far blue line. I was skating behind him, going top speed, trying to catch up. I thought to myself, *Okay, now I see what everyone is talking about.*

It was incredible how smooth his skating was. He did all these little things, and his skates were customized to his exact measurements, and they were also sharpened a special way. I realized that there was a real science to the way Paul skated and how he worked at it. It was no accident that he was a wonderful skater. I learned everything I could from watching him.

Later on in my pro career, I realized that my playing days were coming to an end. As a veteran, I'd grown into a role, taking younger players aside and going over drills and helping them. I enjoyed that. When I was done playing, I wanted to stay in the game and had an opportunity to coach right after I retired as a player. Towards the end of my playing career, I knew I wanted to stay in the game. I got an opportunity to coach in the pro lower levels. This was the start to my second career in hockey.

It wasn't the NHL, that's for sure. I was coaching in a league called the WHA2, a lower-level minor pro league. The team was called the Orlando Seals. Guys were barely making $500 a week. At that rate, you know they were playing for the love of the game. Because of all my years in the minors, I could relate to the players. I had many of the same experiences, both good and bad. I had empathy for what these players were going through. Sharing my story helped the players realize they are not alone.

After two years, Greg Ireland gave me a chance to coach with him in Grand Rapids, the Red Wings' AHL team. I stayed there for nine years. I was happy in Grand Rapids, and at the time I wasn't thinking about coaching internationally. Meanwhile, I have always had relationships with people over in Korea. There is a small hockey community in South Korea, and people knew about me. I had run hockey clinics there and I had some friends there. Right before the Olympics in 2014, the South Korean Olympic Committee contacted me and asked if I wanted to coach the national team to prepare them for the 2018 Olympics. I always wondered why they didn't contact me sooner, but the timing was right, in my opinion. I was more educated in coaching the game and confident in the type of coach I wanted to be. That was a tough decision because my family was settled in Grand Rapids. My wife and I were married thirteen years and we had a daughter, eleven, and son, nine, at the time I accepted the position of Korean National Team coach to prepare for the 2018 Winter Olympics in Korea. It was hard to uproot a young family to an unknown world, but my wife reminded me of a goal my father and I had to be a part of hockey in my homeland.

I had a good job as a part of the Detroit Red Wings organization.

Plus, I still had a year left on my contract. However, something inside of me said, *You better go.*

Grand Rapids and the Red Wings were very supportive. They told me flat out, "Go ahead, Jim, this is a once-in-a-lifetime opportunity." I got blessings from my wife, too. She said to me, "You'd be crazy not to take the job!"

I'd always dreamed of being a part of Korean hockey. Now, as a coach, I'd get to face the world's best teams on an Olympic stage.

There was a lot of work to do. When I first took over, I realized I had to make some changes. To say Korea was an underdog team would be putting it mildly. But I didn't want to hear anyone in the organization say, "Well, we are South Korea, we are twenty-third in the world." To me, that attitude was unacceptable. I wanted them to believe they belonged. We had to change the culture. I got my boss to buy into my plan and give me full rein over the team and the program.

To start, I sourced better equipment. That seems like a small thing, but I had to get my players thinking like they were a top team. We spent a lot of money making sure the players had the best equipment. We also spent a lot of time trying to develop these kids into a high-level hockey team. Practices could be tricky. I speak some Korean, enough to get my point across. But the players had to communicate in Korean, English, Konglish (a hybrid of English and Korean), and hockey talk. Hockey language is all in English, and it doesn't translate into Korean. When I would say things like, "F1, F2, forecheck and backcheck," it only worked in English. We had translators, but they couldn't understand at the time what the hockey terms meant. Also, when you have a translator, it takes the wind out of yelling and screaming at your players. So the players had to learn the hockey terminology I use.

Pretty quickly, we found a way to communicate. There were guys on the team that understood hockey terms and my English, and they helped to communicate the ideas and tereminology to the other players. The basics were easy; the finer details of why we did things was more difficult to explain. Instead of telling a player, "Just go stand there," I had to explain why he had to stand there and why he had to be in a certain position on the ice. That took some time, but it came together.

I found I used a lot of the lessons I learned playing in the NHL and playing for the Penguins. Guys like Wayne Gretzky and Mario Lemieux, they saw the game differently from the rest of us.

I could never see it the way they could. But I could use some of their tendencies and things they did as teaching tools. When I was with Grand Rapids, I'd attend Red Wings training camp. I would watch Pavel Datsyuk and Henrik Zetterberg, how they trained and practiced. I learned a great deal from watching them, from the fact they were always the hardest workers and to the little details they executed in practice and were able to transfer into games. They are unicorns, and what they did on the ice you cannot teach. However, their work ethic, attention to detail, and their preparation, that was something that I could teach.

I took all of that and passed it along to my players. What I've learned mostly from watching these elite players is, ultimately, there is no big secret to being good. It takes a lot of hard work, and those players worked extremely hard.

In the 1991–1992 season, playing for the Penguins, we didn't practice much. Scotty Bowman, our coach, didn't make it a priority. When we did, Scotty almost never came on the ice—he was the bench boss. But we were all in great shape. I have never seen guys ride the stationary bike more than I did in Pittsburgh that year. We had so much talent and depth and leadership on that team, and Scotty didn't need practices to understand how to manage all that talent. He knew exactly when to change things up and do different things to keep us sharp. And he had a really eclectic bunch of guys to work with, that's for sure. I learned a lot from playing for Scotty, about the science of managing players and managing a team. Scotty was a genius on how he thought about the game, and he always managed to put his players in situations to succeed.

The players did a great job of learning from me. When I first arrived, they were like sponges, because they never had coaching of that level before. No matter what I did and what I taught them, they wanted more. They wanted to get better. To get better you have to play against the best. We were able to set up matches against countries that they had never played before, like Canada and the Czech Republic. It didn't matter if we lost. They needed to see and experience up close and in person what league they were in, who they'd have to learn how to beat. I was truly blessed to have the freedom to make my own decisions, which allowed me to make adjustments and develop. I was also blessed with the quality of the players I had that allowed us to improve in such a short period of time. Our improvement gave me the hope to grow Korean hockey and the players' belief that they can be a competitive hockey country.

The experience gained by playing the top teams allowed us to see how those countries played and why they are top teams. Korea has never been able to play at that caliber of competition. So those games prepared us. We have to see it to believe it. The Korean players are NHL fans, too. I remember playing Canada and we got scored on. Our players were excited to see such great players and they were cheering for them.

All of the hard work we put into the program finally paid off when we went into the top division at the World Hockey Championships, Division 1A, playing in Ukraine. We played them once in a Euro

Challenge. Then we played them in the World Championships in Ukraine. It was a tough game that went into shootouts. Our player Shanghoon Shin went down and scored, giving us the opportunity to go up and play in the top division, where we have never gone before.

That was a big step for us. When we beat Ukraine to finally make the top sixteen teams, I told my players, "We have something special here. We have done something that is like a miracle in hockey." When we won that game, I never cried so much in my life. The players had put in the work and really pushed themselves. We had accomplished something totally new in Korean hockey. It was very exciting. Nobody ever thought we could do it, but the players put it all together and they did the unthinkable.

The Korean media and the sports reporters were very positive after we advanced to the top division and were headed to the Olympics. People were at the airport, waiting for us when we arrived in Seoul. That was a whole new experience for us, and it was fantastic having that kind of exposure.

The next step was the actual Olympic Games themselves. I didn't expect to win any medals, and I was hopeful we might win one game. But I knew we would not embarrass ourselves, like a lot of people thought we would, and that would be a success.

On February 15, 2018, we played our first opponent, the Czech Republic. There was a buzz in the air that night. We had prepared a long time for this. We played a lot of these teams preparing for the Olympics and my players understood what I wanted, and they understood my game plan. I still think about that game to this day—we should have won. We scored a goal 5-on-5, but the Czech Republic scored a shorthanded goal and a power-play goal, to beat us 2–1. We were the better team, but our special teams let us down.

We were playing against teams featuring players with multimillion-dollar contracts. I had a team of players who grew up in South Korea and started out with limited skills and opportunities. We continued to compete hard, but Switzerland beat us in our second game and then Canada beat us 4–0. On February 20, in our final game, Finland beat us 5–2. We hadn't won any games, but I thought we had a successful Olympics.

After we lost that final game, as a sign of respect, all the players skated by and bowed to me while I stood on the bench. I will never, ever forget that moment. I still get teary-eyed just thinking about that night.

Those guys put so much effort into it and they sacrificed so much in those four years leading up to the Olympics. I came to Korea in 2014 and my family joined me in 2016 to stay in Korea.

I totally respect what the players did. They are all champions in my eyes.

After the game, speaking to a reporter, I said that South Korea had "just won the gold medal."

What the South Korean team accomplished and where we ended up, to me, was worthy of the gold. Our showing during the 2018 Olympics was a proud moment for Korea, its national team, and me and my family, especially for my mother back in Toronto. All her friends were boasting to her about her son. My mom loved that, and so did my siblings.

I am very blessed to have my family as a part of my life. Without them, I wouldn't have been able to accomplish anything. Everyone was very supportive and cheering for us, and some of my ex-teammates were asking me where they could get a Team South Korea hockey jersey. I made some great friends in hockey, and they followed what I was doing and wanted me to win, except when I played Team Canada! That's okay, I get it.

I would love to coach at the top level, in the NHL, one day. It is all about getting an opportunity.

Someone has to show some confidence and give you the opportunity. I'm hopeful. I have a lot of international experience and I have a lot of North American experience. I am constantly learning and adapting to new systems and the new generation of players. I am also learning how to treat this new generation of player.

After coaching the Korean national team, my vision in hockey has broadened. In international hockey, you see the world's best players, and the level of hockey is fantastic. My hope for the players that went through that experience with me in 2018 is that they'll pass on what they've learned. Maybe some will become coaches themselves in South Korea. I want them to take what they learned and start to lead younger kids to get them into the game. The better we get at grooming the U18 and U20 teams in South Korea, the better future we will have for the national team.

For South Korean hockey to continue to grow, it needs to happen that way. That is why that international hockey experience is so important. I know a lot is said about the current culture in hockey and some of the issues the sport is dealing with off the ice. My experiences have always been good, though. Honestly, hockey players are always complaining about something. But once you retire from playing, you realize how much time was spent complaining. My friend Jeff Chychrun told me that was one thing he regrets is not appreciating it all more at the time, because it is a wonderful sport and look at what it has given us.

Twenty-five years after we won the Cup in 1991 with the Penguins, we all got together for a reunion. Not one of us talked about goals and plays. We talked about the fun and good times that we had off the ice and in the dressing room. All of that goes beyond fame and money.

I am a firm believer that if you chase your passion, the money will come. We all played because we loved the game so much. We played hurt and we sacrificed because we loved the sport and we wanted to be a part of it. We wanted to contribute to our team, no matter what.

Hockey is changing. The sport is recognizing ability regardless of colour or race or gender. I think people in the hockey world are appreciating knowledge of the game more and more. When I broke into the NHL, it was a different game back then. It was mainly dominated by middle-class white kids. I wasn't a superstar, but I found my place. I think of the discipline that I learned, the amazing relationships we forged, and the sacrifices we all made—all of those life skills are found in this wonderful sport, no matter what role you play on the team.

What other sport but hockey has all of this excitement? We get to do so much and travel the world and experience so many great things. Thanks to hockey, I won the Stanley Cup twice, got my picture in the newspaper with Mario Lemieux, made many lifelong friends, and coached a team in the Olympics.

Many people will look at my NHL career and say I was successful, and I was. But I think about those players on the South Korean national team, what they learned and fought through and overcame and accomplished, and I think hockey can offer success for anyone.

11

Healing Through Hockey

Marian Jacko

When you look at the statistics in Canada, Indigenous women are twelve times more likely to be murdered than anyone else in this country. For me, it is about changing the narrative for these young women.

———

I said in a meeting recently that my dream would be to say that Indigenous women and girls are twelve times more likely to play professional women's hockey.

I honestly believe we can change that narrative through hockey. I see what hockey has given to me and my daughters and I see the values and the life lessons that hockey can teach you. I have learned many things in life, and one of them is that hockey can do so much good.

I am a current member of the Hockey Canada Board of Directors. A longtime lawyer, I am the assistant deputy attorney general for the Indigenous Justice division of the Ontario Ministry of the Attorney General. I am also a proud Anishinaabe from Wiikwemkoong First Nation, located in northeast Manitoulin Island, in northern Ontario.

When I was growing up on Manitoulin Island, I was always interested in playing hockey as a child. But at the time, it wasn't something that was afforded to female hockey players. Hockey was male dominated. I actually didn't start playing hockey until I was an adult and I started playing in a women's recreational league. I never played hockey as a young person or anything at a high level. I only played recreational hockey, and to be quite honest, I don't think I was particularly good.

Even though I didn't play hockey when I was growing up, I always loved hockey. As a child, I remember sitting and watching hockey games with my dad on our old-school black-and-white TV back in the day. As I became an adult and I had children, I tried to get my son involved in hockey. I taught him to skate and all that. He didn't really pick it up and he didn't really have much of an interest. My daughters came along, and I taught my oldest daughter, she's a 2003 birth year, and she picked up on hockey right away and loved it. I was living vicariously through her. My second daughter was born in 2005 and I got her involved in hockey as well. They played from what was then called tyke, and they played all the way up to the U18 level. Once they started playing at the U12 level, they both started playing rep hockey.

Because I was so passionate about hockey and I was so grateful that my daughters were playing, I wanted to be involved. So, I volunteered to be on the bench as a trainer. Eventually I became the coach of a U11 my daughter was on. I really enjoyed the coaching and then I started to take courses on coaching hockey, and I received my certification. I loved the game as a child watching with my dad, and I loved seeing my daughters playing the sport. The fact that I wasn't able to play as a young girl, and then seeing my daughters being able to play, I was so grateful.

I coached my youngest her entire time playing minor hockey. She played at A-level rep hockey, so I had to get knowledgeable about the sport, learning systems and how to coach. I took it upon myself to take some courses and do some of my own self-study.

In all of my coaching experiences, I brought with me and shared with the team, most of whom were not Indigenous, the teachings from my Anishinaabe background. I tried to infuse those teachings into my coaching. For example, I talked to the girls about the beaver and the turtle and the duck in nature. The girls would look at me and say, "What does this have to do with hockey?"

I would tell them the story of the duck. Look at a duck in nature in its natural habitat. It takes the oils from underneath them and puts them on top of the feathers. I would ask them why they do that? The girls would look at me and say, "I don't know." I would explain that when the duck puts the natural oils on top of the feathers, their feathers don't get wet and weigh them down and drown them. This way, the water rolls off its back.

I would tell them, "This is how it translates to hockey. When you are on the ice and someone swears at you or makes a comment about you or you get angry about a missed play or a missed shot, you can play like the duck, let it roll off your back, and not let it bring you down. Your job is to get yourself prepared mentally to be able to ignore the nonsense on the ice and play your game."

As the girls got older, having that mindset helped them avoid those retaliation penalties that hurt a team. I infused the lesson of the duck into coaching wherever I went.

No matter where I coached, at the beginning of each season I would give girls something that I called the playbook. In it were the standard drills we would run at practice and the systems we wanted to play. As well, I would include the lessons of the duck and the teachings of the Seven Grandfathers, so they knew what I was talking about. I would tell the girls it was their responsibility to read the playbook and learn the material. That way, when I introduced those subjects into my coaching, they were more receptive. And it didn't matter what the background of my players, they all eventually understood the lessons I was trying to teach them. I wondered at times if the teachings and the lessons would hit home with the girls. It didn't take long for me to understand that the teachings and the lessons mattered to everyone on the team.

Later in the season, I heard the girls talking to each other on the bench after one of them got into a dustup in the corner. The one girl said, "Remember, you want to play like a duck!" It hit me—oh my God, they are getting it. They are really getting it. That was an enormously proud moment for me.

To this day, I still receive text messages from my players. Sometimes, they will text me that they were watching a hockey game and they saw something that I taught them. It was a special time for me, being able to coach these young women.

In the spring of 2023, in my last year of coaching, I asked my son who is an artist to do a painting for me that would depict my coaching experience. I wanted to create a series of limited-edition prints and give them to my players as a final gift.

He painted a turtle with thirteen separate segments on its shell. The shell speaks to truth and the Thirteen Moons of our culture. He also painted a picture of the girls with their hockey sticks up in the air. He painted a beaver in the water. And of course, he painted two ducks swimming near sweetgrass. Because I would also talk about the teachings of sweetgrass and the twenty-one strands. I would tell them that sweetgrass is made up of a series of strands. Like a hockey team, the strands of sweetgrass are unbreakable if they work together. Alone, they fall into the water. The piece of art was framed and given to each player, and they were really touched by it.

In the fall of 2023, the Little NHL (Native Hockey League) were able to bring an all-Indigenous U15 girls team to the Hayley Wickenheiser hockey tournament. The girls arrived at the opening party wearing their traditional ribbon skirts with such pride and wearing their Little NHL jerseys. It melted my heart when I saw that. Two thousand twenty-four marks the fiftieth anniversary of the Little NHL. Because of my role with Hockey Canada, I am on a leave of absence from the Little NHL. However, I still volunteer to help them behind the scenes.

The fiftieth is going to be more like a festival than just a tournament. The theme for the fiftieth is honouring our water. Because without water there is no life. And without water, there is no ice to play hockey on.

The four pillars of the Little NHL are Respect, Citizenship, Sportsmanship, and Education. It also gives us an opportunity to shine a light on the water crisis going on in First Nations communities across Canada.

How I ended up on the Hockey Canada Board of Directors is an interesting story. My kids are all adults now. When Hockey Canada announced that they were looking for new directors on their board, some people sent me the link with the information. When I told my kids, they said that I should apply.

At first, I thought they were crazy, why would I want to do that? At the time, Hockey Canada's Board of Directors was made up of ten white guys. I didn't think I would fit in. I thought about it some more and did some research, and then I decided to submit my name and apply. I thought the worst that could happen is that they say no. I applied, and I was selected by the nominating committee and my name was put forth as one of the finalists. Lucky for me, I was not elected.

That year, the entire Board of Directors at Hockey Canada had to resign because of a variety of scandals. Had I been selected, I would have been part of that board. I felt like I dodged a bullet, and the Creator is looking out for me. Making sure that I was in the right place at the right time.

The next time Hockey Canada was looking for people to submit their name for the Board of Directors, I decided to go for it. I had applied before and I was passionate about hockey, and I wanted to help, and I knew they were in a real crisis at the time.

With my upbringing and my teachings, I felt strongly that women needed to lead the work to fix things. There was much healing and repairing that needed to be done with Hockey Canada. I also felt like it was an opportunity for me to contribute and give back a little because hockey has given me so much in my life.

When I put my name forth the second time, I was one of the nine members of the interim Board of Directors. I wasn't sure what I was getting myself into. At first, there was a series of marathon meetings. We would meet weekly for at least three hours virtually. Just before the World Juniors, we met in person from 7:30 in the morning until eight o'clock at night. There was just so much to do and so much to discuss. We were really in crisis management mode trying to figure out a better path forward.

One of the teachings I shared with the rest of the board was something I learned when I was young. As much as we were in a hurry to fix things, I reminded everyone what the elders taught us. They would say, "If you have the luxury of time, you should take the time." That way you can think about your decisions and the impact they will have on future generations. We have to be mindful of how our decisions will affect the future generations. The elders would say, "If you move down that path too quickly, you will create dust, and the ones that follow will become lost in that dust."

I reminded everyone of this, and it really resonated with the board members, especially Cassie Campbell-Pascall. She told me she found my words very powerful. It reminded her of her days playing hockey at the Olympics. One of the things the coaches would tell the players at the Olympic level as they would pass the puck and make crisp, tape-to-tape passes, "No dust." That was our mantra during our time on the interim board, "No dust." We have to be careful with our decisions and mindful of the impact of our decisions.

I am so proud of the work that the interim board did. We spent an incredible amount of time and did an incredible amount of work. There was a lot of personal sacrifice from our own families during this time. No matter how much we all sacrificed, it was well worth it, and I would do it again in a heartbeat. I believe in hockey and the value of the sport, and I believe in Hockey Canada.

With my new term on Hockey Canada, I can continue to do the important work we have been doing. And I know from the feedback that I have received we are doing good work, and we are on the right path.

I have had people tell me with tears in their eyes that I have changed their soul. Everybody comes at this from a unique perspective. I haven't had negative feedback at all from my time with Hockey Canada.

While I was on the board with Hockey Canada, I was also on a female hockey policy committee that was chaired by Cassie Campbell-Pascall. I was also part of the CEO search committee. I was very busy, but it was all good work and extremely rewarding.

Hockey is more than just a sport to me. I often tell the story that coaching hockey was a form of self-care for me. I would have the worst day in my job as a lawyer and I would go to the rink and step on the ice with those girls at practice, and all of my troubles would just melt away. I would leave the rink at the end of practice, and I felt rejuvenated. I would always tell my teams; they give me more than I can give them.

Being on the board of Hockey Canada, I can't coach and run a team. That means I don't receive the self-care I would get from coaching my own team. As I mentioned earlier, I also had to take a leave of absence from the Little NHL. The fact that I am willing to step away from coaching, and the fact I stepped away from the Little NHL, speaks volumes in terms of how I feel about the work that needs to be done at Hockey Canada.

When I think about change at Hockey Canada, I think about the difference between a ship versus a speedboat. A speedboat can move really quick, but if you are in a large ship like Hockey Canada, it is going to take a while to get there. But at least now, the ship is on the right course. We are not there yet, but we are heading in the right direction.

In 2023 Hockey Canada hosted a summit on women and girls in hockey. That is where we are seeing the biggest growth in hockey. Now, we have the PWHL (Professional Women's Hockey League).

There was also a summit on toxic masculinity in hockey. As part of that, Hockey Canada retained a professor, and what she did was a literature review and since we were in a safe space, we could have those difficult conversations.

We are in the beginnings of change, and by hosting these various summits, we are ensuring that Hockey Canada is heading in the right direction. I often remind people that we have so many reports and commissions that tell us what the problems are. Now we have to start talking about some of the solutions. Let's make this our act of reconciliation in hockey. Let's do things in the spirit of change. I know we have a lot of allies and a lot of people who are of like mind. There is also a certain percentage of the population who just aren't there yet.

With education and awareness, and by taking one step after another, we can get there. I don't think we can get there in my lifetime, but hopefully if I can help in any small way to improve things for future generations to come, then I will have done my job. The elders say that with the work that you do, you have to think about how you are going to make your ancestors proud. And that is what I think about. When my time on this earth is done, am I going to be able to say that made my ancestors proud? I try to do my best every day, and I'm doing it for my children and my grandchildren and those future generations.

And by using the lessons of our elders, and translating them to hockey, anything is possible. Thanks to those lessons, whenever I am in doubt, I try to act like a duck!

12

A Love of Hockey
and Helping Others

Chix with Stix

*T*here is a group of women in the Windsor, Ontario, area who are among the most dedicated hockey players you will ever meet. They range in age from their thirties to their eighties and are using their passion for hockey to help others. The group is called Chix with Stix, and they are more proof to the saying that age is just a number.

———

Heather Forsyth

I didn't start playing hockey until I was nineteen years old. They let me play on one of the girls house league teams, even though I was too old. I learned to play hockey there from one of the coaches on our team. I had never been on hockey skates before, so I had to relearn how to skate. They let me play that year, even though I was one year too old. Then I played recreational intramural girls hockey while I went to school at St. Clair College. The more I played, the better I got. I was picking up the sport at a pretty fast pace.

Growing up, I always watched hockey. My family is from Toronto, so we were Maple Leafs fans. Considering I grew up in Red Wings country, being a Leafs fan wasn't easy.

After I graduated college, I had nowhere to play hockey. So, I answered an ad in the local paper. This team called Chix with Stix were looking for women hockey players. And the rest is history.

When I first showed up to play with Chix with Stix, I was a little nervous. In the beginning, I was an extra player if they needed someone. Eventually they needed a player to skate with them permanently, and I was in. No matter what, everyone on the team was very nice to me.

Shalaina Kitsos

It was my aunt who started the team. She was married and had four kids who were all playing hockey. Her husband was a coach and her family basically lived at the local arena. She thought, "Hey, if everyone in my family is part of hockey, why can't I do it?" She had zero hockey background, other than always being at the rink with her kids. She found some other women from her husband's work who were interested. Those women asked a friend, and those women asked more friends, and it grew by word of mouth.

At first, all the women used borrowed equipment. Nobody had their own, and nobody came from a hockey-playing background. I was part of the original group, and the only ice time we could get was on Saturday night at 11:30. We were all connected to each other in some way, but we didn't really know each other at first. Six months after we started, we were able to get some consistent ice time, and by this time, it was on Thursday night at 10. Which, for all of us, was pretty late. We have no refs, but we do call each other if someone is offsides. To be honest, it took us years to even start calling offsides. It took a while!

Heather

Not only do we go out after each game, but we get together once a year in the off-season. Every year, we all get together for a big cottage trip. There are about twenty-five of us who get together for a weekend. And we usually have a theme every time we go to the cottage. We have a lot of fun when we are together. We have a goalie who just turned thirty, and our oldest player, Betty, is in her early eighties. In 2023 she went on the disabled list briefly after she blocked a shot. She was eighty-one years old at the time.

Kathleen Rocheleau

I am one of the oldest players. I am in my mid-sixties. Betty and I joined the team around the same time. I started playing and then I asked if Betty could join us. I do have some background in hockey. Working with my husband, I started out teaching children how to skate. We also coached, and my husband worked as a referee. I was the vice president, and then eventually the president of the local hockey association. To top it off, I have five sons who all played hockey as well. However, out of all of my sons and my husband, I am the only one still playing. I have had two full tears in my rotator cuff over the years, and I am still playing hockey.

Shalaina

Nobody messes with Kathleen! Our attitude is tape it up and keep playing. When we can't physically play hockey anymore, we have joked that we are going to start a choir. That way we can still be together.

Heather

Hockey is a fantastic way to relieve all our stress and just laugh. In some ways, it isn't even about the hockey. We just love getting together and joking around. There are times I have more fun on the bench than I do on the ice. There are times when the stories are so good, I can't wait for shift to end so I can get back to the stories on the bench and all of the laughs. We saw a story that in women's sports, a lot of women stopped playing during Covid and never went back.

Shalaina

But we all came back!

Heather

During Covid, we would still hold get-togethers. We'd go to Betty's house, our eighty-year-old player, and we'd sit outside in our lawn chairs and make sure everyone was six feet apart. We usually had a backyard fire going and we would all just hang out and enjoy each other's company. Not only do we support each other off the ice, but we also do a lot of fundraising as a team. In 2023, we were part of the Play for a Cure cancer charity.

Kathleen

One of the players on our team raised the most money out of all the girls, and she got to play with the pros. She was a little nervous and she is a mediocre player. When she started out, she was a C-minus-level player, and now, she is at least a B-minus player. But because of her fundraising, she played with the pros and got to do a penalty shot on the goalie. It was a fun game, and she had a blast. The tournament ended up raising over $400,000 for Play for a Cure. There were at least eight of us from Chix with Stix that were a part of that team.

Heather

A few of the older children of some of the women will come out and skate with us. The younger ones are too good for us! However, there are times when we have people who are missing and some of the women will bring their young kids out to play.

Shalaina

I have two teenage daughters who play house league hockey. I have always told them that my only hope is that one day, when you are done playing organized hockey, that you find a group like I found. Because it is more than a place to play hockey, it is a support group as well. It is a good place to be, and you are with people who you can lean on.

Heather

In the summer of 2023, a group of us were a part of the City of Windsor Council on Aging. Kathleen was a part of the 3-on-3 hockey for Easter Seals in the fall of 2023.

Kathleen

When we took part in the Play for a Cure event, we got to play with two great players. Because our team raised more money than any of the other girls teams, we drafted Meghan Agosta and Laura Fortino. They are Canadian Olympic players, and they were great. Their skating was smooth, they were gliding all over the ice effortlessly.

Heather

My mom was organizing a walk for aging, and she talked about our team. Age should never stop you from doing what you love. The local CBC channel heard about us, and they did a story about our team. They loved our story. We were becoming internet stars!

Shalaina

I had a friend in London call me and tell me he heard about our team and the story the CBC had done on us.

Kathleen

Our eighty-year-old was on the disabled list after blocking that shot, but she was so determined to get back to playing with us. She went to public skating, and she felt weird without her stick. This was a public skating for seniors, and I asked the organizers if Betty could bring her stick. They said it was fine. So, they let us use our hockey sticks as our canes on the ice!

Heather

When you stop, that is when you slow down. That is why none of us want to stop playing hockey.

A mutual friend of the women from Chix with Stix is Jody Christian. Hailing from the Windsor suburb of Tecumseh, Christian is an important member of a group of volunteers helping kids who otherwise couldn't afford to play hockey. The group is called Knobby's Kids, and without them, hundreds of kids from the Windsor area might never get a chance to learn how to skate or how to play hockey.

Jody Christian

I played Senior AA women's hockey in Sarnia before I moved to Windsor. I played for the Sarnia Sting Senior AA women's team, which is good considering that I didn't start playing hockey until I was sixteen years old. Back when I was young, they didn't have girls hockey, so I had to be a figure skater until I started playing hockey. What happened was that when I turned sixteen, I was able to drive. I played in Wallaceburg, Ontario, with some girls who were older than me. When I was twenty-one, I started playing competitive hockey in Sarnia. I was a late bloomer.

When I am not playing hockey, I build minivans at the Stellantis plant in Windsor.

I coached one year of university hockey at the University of Windsor. That was tough, trying to juggle a full-time job and work as an assistant coach at the university level. I was the defensive coach, that was in the late nineties and the University of Windsor women's hockey program wasn't established yet. Despite the challenges, I learned more as a player that year, coaching those girls, than I had in all of my previous years of hockey.

When I was done after my one year at the University of Windsor, I took a break from hockey. Then one day, I was reading the *Windsor Star* newspaper, and I found an article on Knobby's Kids. There was a picture of two kids with the headline "Knobby's Kids." They were two little girls, toothless grins, and they looked so happy with their helmets and facemasks on. After reading the article I called up the organization and I asked them, "Do you have women mentors on the ice coaching the girls that are in the program?"

They said, "Actually, no, we don't." I told them, "I would love to come out and mentor these young girls." I told them I volunteer with Big Sisters, and it is a wonderful experience. I was hoping to pass on my hockey passion to these little girls. That was back in 2012 and I have been a volunteer coach at Knobby's Kids ever since.

Knobby's Kids started in 2006. It all takes place on an outdoor rink. Because of that, we have a very short season. We typically start in early December, and we are done by the first week of March.

We started the 2023–2024 season in the second weekend of December and the ice was beginning to melt at the end of our sessions. But it sure beats skating outside when it is minus 20!

I didn't get to play hockey as a young girl, and when I did play, it was always one of the dads who coached us. I never had that female coach until I was in my late thirties. I never had a female mentor and I kind of missed that. By mentoring these young girls at Knobby's Kids I can make sure they have a female who is coaching them, and, at the same time, I can have fun with the sport.

I want to show them that hockey can be fun. We don't always have to play to make the NHL. We want to be out there, playing hockey and having fun. I want these kids to dream, because they are kids, but have fun doing it. The best part of Knobby's Kids is that there are no parents yelling at us. It is all about letting kids be kids and allowing them to try the sport.

I tell the kids that I coach, and I tell my nephews, it's great to score goals, because that is how you win games. But I am proudest when I see you get an assist and set up someone else to score. When you play hockey, you should never just go out there thinking that you have to score goals. You have to get assists and get your teammates involved in the game.

In the 2023–2024 season, we have a record number of kids taking part in Knobby's Kids, with a total of 170 signed up. In previous years, when times were tough, there were kids' families who couldn't afford the cost of organized hockey and a lot of them ended up playing with us. But this year is the busiest we have seen it. We had to cap it off at 170 kids because we only have three hours of ice a week. While it isn't great, if we didn't provide those three hours, 170 kids wouldn't have been able to play hockey.

We have a diverse city in Windsor and the surrounding area, and we have a lot of newcomers. A lot of those newcomers, kids who don't speak much English, are part of Knobby's Kids this year. But you don't need to speak a lot when we are on the ice. I tend to get the kids who look like Bambi on ice and have never skated before. On our first day of the season, I had thirty kids who had never skated before. My favourite moment took place later that first day. I had two eleven-year-old twins who I was working with, I looked at them and said, "You're twins, right?" And they said, "Oh yeah." Well, they were taller than me and I am five foot, ten inches tall. Neither one of them had been on skates before. They were all smiles and so happy to be out there. But they were both natural athletes, and at the end of the hour they were already practicing their inside edges and skating around. I was so proud of them, and they would only get better. That's why I coach, for moments like that.

When you turn sixteen, you age out of our program. A lot of those kids will come back and help me, and that way they get the volunteer hours that they need to graduate in high school in Ontario. We can't have too many people on the ice helping, but it's great to have kids who used to be in the program and then return and give back. One day, there was a little boy who was crying, and he didn't want to try and skate. The dad said to him, "Come on, just try it. Your dad went through this program when he was a little boy." I was so emotional when I heard that. The son was following in his father's skates and being a part of Knobby's Kids.

There are three older guys who originally created Knobby's Kids back in 2006. These were men who were active in the Windsor community. Knobby's is too big to be run by one person. It takes a team to run it, and I am proud to be a part of that team.

We are at the point now that we do breakfast for the kids every three weeks. We hand out presents to the kids at Christmas. We have this lovely administrator named Liz, and the kids have to check in with Liz every time they play, and we give out awards at the end of the season for perfect attendance. We give out awards to the most dedicated player. And then there is Joe; he is in his late seventies and he is our dedicated equipment manager. He brings a truck and trailer to the outdoor rink with extra equipment if someone has broken equipment. The community had donated most of our equipment and if we have more than we need, we donate it to a local Indigenous reserve. I have a friend who is a local teacher, and they needed some helmets so the kids could play floor hockey in gym class. We had extra helmets, so we donated a bunch to him.

I have so much fun with Knobby's Kids. Competitive coaching can be incredibly stressful and it is very serious business. What I do now is total fun and that is a feeling that I want to pass on to the kids, that hockey is fun. A number of the kids go on to play organized minor hockey. In fact, Knobby's Kids sponsors two of our kids every year, paying for their minor hockey fees.

I had a young mother say to me this week, "Emily just *loves* you, she loves coming to hockey and seeing you. She has so much fun every week.

My whole goal is that by the time March rolls around and we are at the end of the season, my thirty Bambi-on-ice beginners have graduated to the other end of the ice, doing drills with more skilled kids. When that happens, I actually shed a tear. They are my little protégés, and I love to see how far they have come in one season.

I still play pickup hockey on Tuesday nights. No refs, but we set up even teams and we still have a really good skate every week. I do that Tuesdays and Sundays. It is amazing the connections that you make through hockey. I have a friend who has some acquaintances in Michigan. They had asked her to play in this tournament for women fifty years of age and older. They asked her if she knew another woman in that age group who was a fairly decent hockey player. The event is very competitive, and my friend Val asked me to join her, and we ended up taking part in the Michigan Senior Olympics. We were called the Geri-Hat-tricks, and we won three gold medals in our division.

I love playing hockey and I want to keep playing hockey as long as I can. Winning a hockey game is great, but nothing makes me happier than to see the look on a kid's face when they realize that they have learned how to skate. At that moment, you just know they have developed a lifelong love of hockey.

13

Hockey Dreams in Canada

Sunaya Sapurji

The lights at the Gord and Irene Risk Arena in Toronto would come on early in the evening. We lived on the seventh floor of an apartment building and my bedroom window had a clear view of the ice. At the time, when I was a child, it was still an outdoor rink. When I couldn't sleep, skaters would provide my entertainment at all hours of the night, especially late when the ice time was cheapest.

Before cell phones and laptops, this was my nightly distraction and there was something soothing about watching a lone skater outside in the cold from the comfort of my warm bed. And it always felt fitting. I grew up loving hockey, though no one in my family could understand why.

My parents met and married in England and, when I was four, we all emigrated to Canada. Despite my grandparents and extended family still living in the United Kingdom, my parents, like many other immigrants, came to Canada in search of better opportunities. It wasn't the first time they'd travelled looking for something better. My father grew up in India and left for England, where he had extended family, by himself as a sixteen-year-old. It took him nineteen days to make the trip from Mumbai to Tilbury, London, on the RMS *Orion*. My mother was born and raised in the port of Aden, in current-day Yemen, when it was still a British colony. Her family left for England when war broke out.

Neither of them had much experience with ice or snow, let alone hockey. But my dad has always been a huge sports fan. He loves tennis, soccer, cricket, horse racing, and motorsports. He's been to every grand slam tennis event at least once, attended two Olympic Games, countless cricket test matches, and several World Cups, including in 1966 when England won on home soil. Many of my favourite childhood memories are of me sitting with my dad either in front of the TV or at various sporting events. One of my earliest memories is of me, my mom, and sister huddling around our TV and waiting for the local sports segment on Citytv because Dad was interviewed in a "fan on the street" segment after John McEnroe beat Bjorn Borg in Toronto at the Molson Challenge.

My mom was very no-nonsense and into girl power long before the Spice Girls existed. For her, raising me and my younger sister meant letting us know that nothing was off-limits just because we were women. And she was someone who put her thoughts into action every day in the way she carried herself and interacted with the world. "Don't ever let anyone tell you that you can't do something," she would say.

Dad's passion for sports definitely passed down to me, but I came to love hockey out of necessity. Growing up, there weren't too many girls to play with in my parents' circle of friends. Most of the kids my age were boys who were into hockey. The Maple Leafs were their team of choice and in order to survive, I had to learn as much if not more about the team. We would play a game where someone would say a number and you'd have to list all the players in the NHL who wore it. The other game was to take turns naming a player on the Leafs roster until someone couldn't, making them the loser. The Miroslavs—Frycer and Ihnacak—were always my go-to if I found myself in trouble.

If I knew we were going to visit an aunt or uncle on the weekend (in the Parsi community, we often call friends of the family aunty or uncle as a sign of respect even if they aren't related), I'd watch all the hockey I could on TV or devour the *Toronto Star* sports section for the latest NHL news. It became a regular part of my routine, and I genuinely grew to love it.

We spent many Christmases at the home of my uncle Dinshaw and his wife, Gool. They had a big split-level place in Ajax, Ontario, and there would be a large group of friends who would all go on Christmas morning and stay overnight. All the kids would bring their sleeping bags and camp out in the living room so we could get up early and watch cartoons and the World Junior Championships.

At that point, I started watching any and all kinds of hockey. The OHL Game of the Week was a regular weekend feature on Global TV and became appointment viewing. I had no idea where Sault Ste.

Marie or Owen Sound was, but it all sounded very exotic when I was a kid.

I remember clearly one intermission segment that featured Toronto Marlboros defenceman Brian Collinson—who I guess liked to paint in his spare time—being interviewed about his art. They showed a few of his paintings, but I only remember a sailboat. In hindsight, what came next likely changed the course of my life. There was an outro telling viewers they could get Marlies tickets for $2 at their local Becker's convenience store for their games at Maple Leaf Gardens.

Maple Leaf Gardens was something out of a fairy tale. Even though we lived in Toronto, I had only experienced that place on TV from the living room of our apartment. Admittedly, I was a very lucky child, because my dad would regularly take me and my sister to sporting events. We'd go to Blue Jays games, I'd pick his "winners" at Woodbine Racetrack, and there was even an ill-fated trip to the International Centre to watch the first Wrestlemania, with my future brother-in-law and his father, who is one of my dad's best friends. It was a disaster. I'm not sure what our dads were expecting; it was wrestling after all. We were told to never speak of it again.

"Dad, you have to take me to a Marlies game," I begged him. "It's $2 and I have $2 to pay for my ticket. Please."

"What? Come on, Sunaya, how could you like this goon sport?" he responded.

Whenever hockey was brought up, my dad would tease me by calling it a goon sport. To be fair, back in the 1980s when I was still in my formative hockey-watching years, he was not all that wrong.

Still, we went to Becker's and bought our tickets. We took the TTC down to Maple Leaf Gardens and sat in the green section. During the intermission, I wandered the concourse taking in the Gardens in all its glory. When the game was over—a Marlies win over the Oshawa

Generals—an usher asked if we were going to stay for the Leafs practice. I thought he was joking, but at the time, a ticket for the Marlboros would get you in to see the Leafs practice. After that experience, we started going to games more frequently.

I was a Leafs fan growing up, but two things changed that. The first was game 4 of the best-of-seven Norris Division semifinal against the Detroit Red Wings in 1988, where the Leafs lost 8–0 and fans pelted the ice with debris. (This was during the John Brophy era, so the "Brophy's Boys" hats were a popular item on the ice along with jerseys.) It was soul-crushing.

Soon after, in 1989, the decision was made to not re-sign Borje Salming, my favourite player, who instead joined Detroit as a free agent. So, I went with Borje to the Red Wings and never looked back.

Thanks to my dad's job at Multimatic, a global automotive supplier, he had a line on Red Wings tickets. When I was old enough to drive, some friends from high school and I would pile into a car and drive to Detroit for the occasional afternoon game.

At that point, hockey had become an obsession. I knew I wanted to be involved in sports, and becoming a reporter seemed like the best way for me to reach that goal. Since my interest in hockey went well beyond the NHL, I would often listen to York University games on the radio. When I was in high school, we moved to Woodbridge, a Toronto suburb, and the signal from York's campus community radio station 105.5 FM would easily reach my Walkman. They would play PSAs looking for volunteers, so even before I went to York for school I was volunteering at the radio station, CHRY. I started in the news department because there were no openings at the time in sports.

The radio station, being mostly volunteer-run and reliant on donations, had really old equipment. It had old everything. The walls in Vanier College, where the station resided, were almost completely covered with band posters, flyers, and assorted ephemera. The carpet was threadbare for a long time until a local company was kind enough to offer us some industrial carpeting no one else wanted. In my early days there, you would have been hard-pressed to find a chair that wasn't broken. Station managers Gary Wright and Stephe Perry did their best to keep the place afloat, and there was a lovable charm about it. At a time when people were using computers, CHRY was still reliant on typewriters for preparing scripts.

"How many words a minute can you type?" asked news director Denyse Stewart.

"I'm not sure, I don't really type a lot," I said. The truth was, I couldn't type. At all.

"You're going to have to come in earlier or learn to type faster," said Stewart.

It was here I met some of my best friends and learned firsthand about the business of reporting. Working at CHRY changed my life in many ways, exposing me to a diversity of both people and thought. Looking back on it now, it might have served me much better than if I had gone the more traditional journalism school route (my degree was in English and mass communications). I don't think Stewart or assistant news director Nadira Baksh realized the impact they had on me at the station; truth be told, I probably didn't realize it myself at the time. Having two women of colour to mentor me and, more importantly, challenge me and my views on the world at large was a gift for which I am still grateful. It was a welcoming place for a young, extremely naive reporter, and I never felt discouraged or anything other than empowered while I was there.

I spent an inordinate amount of time at the radio station—often skipping classes. Eventually, there was an opening in the sports department and I took over one of the weekday spots of the 5:55 sports report, which was a recap of the day's top sports stories. I also started volunteering as the scorekeeper/stats person on the station's broadcasts of York men's hockey, with former CBC reporter Mel Broitman doing the play-by-play and Ted Rechtshaffen, who among other things now writes a financial column at the *National Post*, doing colour commentary. Most of our games were called out of the Ice Palace, the old arena on the York grounds. It was aptly named. That building was so cold most nights I'd write stats in pencil because the ink would freeze in pens.

Eventually, I'd spent enough time at the radio station (cutting a lot of classes) to become the sports editor there. That meant I was in charge of setting up all our York U sports broadcasts. We covered hockey, basketball, football, and even ventured into volleyball. My three main jobs for those broadcasts were to make sure we had a dedicated phone line for the broadcast, find a board operator, and lug our equipment and set it up wherever it needed to go. All the equipment— the mixer, cables and headsets, and mics—was kept in an old marble green suitcase from the forties or fifties everyone called "Atlantic City." One day I asked why the name.

"Because it looks like the kind of suitcase movie mobsters would carry in Atlantic City," Ted replied. "A good suitcase for carrying the loot."

When the station had enough money to purchase a remote mic, I became the in-game reporter, getting injury updates from talking to coaches during intermission, and speaking to people in the stands. We covered some good teams led by longtime head coach Graham Wise. During that time, I met several people in the hockey world I'd cross paths with again at different times in my career, including two former York captains, Mike Futa and Jim Hulton.

Even though our sports department was small and almost entirely volunteer-run—I think I was paid a weekly stipend of $50 as sports director—we had some excellent talent who would go on to do big things in media, including baseball broadcaster Hazel Mae, communications executive Andrea Goldstein, TV producer Miriam Elmaleh, sports broadcaster Trevor Thompson, and Rob Gillies, who started as a high school co-op student at CHRY and is now the bureau chief for the Associated Press in Canada.

The radio station was my gateway to covering junior hockey. There were many student athletes at York, and Nathan LaFayette, who would go on to play in the NHL, was one of them. At the time he was playing for the Newmarket Royals, and when he returned from winning gold at the 1993 World Juniors he was a guest on the afternoon sports show I was hosting at the station. I had contemplated doing an OHL show, but I wasn't sure if it would be a good fit for our audience. So, after our interview, I asked Nathan what he thought.

"I think you should do it," he said.

"Yeah, but what if no one listens?"

"Who cares?" he replied.

And that short, throwaway conversation was the start of my decades-long journey covering junior hockey.

I started hosting *The OHL Report* during our Tuesday afternoon sports slot. I'd interview players, coaches, and executives and run down the latest news from the league. One of the first people I met in the league was Larry Mavety, who was head coach and GM of the Belleville Bulls. I drove to Belleville to do a story on then-rookie Dan Cleary and his linemates Craig Mills and Brian Secord. Mav was a larger-than-life character who had been an extra in *Slap Shot*, having played pro hockey for years in the IHL, WHL, and WHA. To a young reporter, he was an intimidating figure: a big man with a booming, deep, gravelly voice. He could not have been more helpful, inviting me into his office to talk and making sure everyone I needed spoke to me before I left. Later on, when I covered the league full-time, I used to joke with him that maybe if he had been more of a jerk, I would have switched to covering a different sport. We kept in touch even after he retired from the day-to-day of the OHL. I could always count on his advice. Mav passed away in December 2020, and there are still days I want to call him up and pick his brain or get his opinion. I miss him a lot.

While at York I also began covering the Junior A Markham Waxers for the *Markham Economist & Sun* newspaper. Travelling on the bus regularly with the team was an education in itself. I covered my first full-scale brawl when the Waxers were on the road to play the Lindsay Muskies. Both teams started fighting in the pregame warm-up before the referee or linesmen were even on the ice. By the time the refs got out there—they weren't even fully dressed—everyone, including some parents, the off-ice officials, and coaches, was on the ice fighting or trying to break up fights. The game eventually went on as scheduled, but once it was over the police were there to escort us onto the bus and then travelled with us until we were well on the road back to Markham.

After graduating, I started a part-time job at Global TV working on their nightly sports show *Sportsline* with Jim Tatti and Gene Principe. From there I answered a newspaper ad looking for someone who was interested in writing about sports. There was no employer listed. Eventually, I got a call for an interview and learned it was for a new venture run by the *Toronto Star*. Being so fresh out of school, the idea of landing a job at the *Star*, the paper I had grown up reading, was a long shot. My expectations were so low, I wasn't even nervous walking into One Yonge Street (where their office was for many years). With that in mind, I met with Phil Bingley, who was the *Star*'s deputy managing editor, and for an hour we just talked about sports. No one was more surprised than I was when Phil called to say the job was mine.

It was a contract job, *Sports Pick*, kind of like ProLine meets NTN. The idea was well ahead of its time. It was on the nineteenth floor of the *Star* Building and had a big working bar—with tables, chairs, projection TV, and beer on tap—in a room called "The Lab" because it was where market research was conducted. My job was essentially to write some of the sports text for the game and to edit ticker-type sports news for when the system was up and running. It was a motley crew of fun and talented people and it lasted about a year before the *Star* pulled the plug.

Out of work, I ended up putting my degree to use working at a marketing and communications agency run by one of my former co-workers at *Sports Pick*. I did that for a while before fate intervened. The *Toronto Star* was expanding its internet presence and looking for copy editors to work in sports. One day on my way home from work, Phil saw me on the streetcar. He didn't say anything to me (and I didn't notice him at the time) but seeing me prompted him to later send an email asking if I might be interested in coming back.

Much like hockey, you not only need skill and tenacity to make it in media, but opportunity and someone who believes in you, too. For me, Phil was always that guy. Going back to the *Star* this time, I was a copy editor on the web side of the sports department; but given my background in junior hockey they asked if I'd take over the weekly OHL notebook.

In 2000, when I started at the *Star,* there were very few women in sports, let alone covering junior hockey. And certainly no women of colour. When I moved from the web to the newspaper side of the editing desk, I was often the only woman there, too. But we had Mary

Ormsby as the assistant sport editor; she was someone who served as a role model for me and many others in the business. She was one of the women waging locker room battles to help make it a little easier for people like me. She was also a working mom, and married to the wonderful hockey writer Paul Hunter, so it was important for me to see that I could have those things, too, if I wanted.

The sports desk at the *Star* was probably the most fun I've ever had on the job. Many of the people there were newspaper veterans who had been talented writers in their own right. The sports department was on the opposite side of the newsroom where we had TVs to watch games at night. People brought in snacks, and there was always shouting and laughing. Others around the newsroom would wander over to see what was happening. It was our own little fiefdom. So, I'd work at night on the sports desk and use my days and nights off to watch and write about junior hockey.

People often ask me what it is about the junior game I enjoy so much. It's never a simple answer. Part of it is the community it builds. Another part is the access to people and their time, getting to write about players before they become household names. And part of it is that it's not perfect. In junior, players are always making mistakes, so it's anything but predictable. That goes for off the ice, too.

One time covering a game at St. Michael's College School Arena where the OHL Majors were playing, I had gone down early to interview Mississauga IceDogs forward Cody Bass. Walking through the lower bowl, I was stopped by the Majors PR person Parker Neale.

"Don't go up to the press box," he said.

He looked flustered.

"Is everything okay?" I asked.

"No," he said. "There's a raccoon in the press box. I had to fight it off with a chair, so it's probably angry. It scared the life out of me."

"Are you serious?" I asked in disbelief. "A raccoon! In the press box?"

"Animal Control is on the way, so just be careful."

Calling it a "press box" is generous since it was more like a steel scaffolding in one corner of the rink that was completely open save for some railings. (Sitting up there during warm-up was a death trap because pucks hitting the crossbar could come flying up at full speed.) As Bass and I were talking, I could see the people from Animal Control trying to corral the raccoon. We had to stop the interview because it was both surreal and hilarious since the raccoon managed to jump onto the protective netting behind the glass before finally being captured.

I spent the majority of those early years at the *Star* covering the St. Michael's Majors, who were one of the newer franchises in the league. Living downtown at the time made it easy for me to get to games, and there was a lot to write about—mostly chaos. It wasn't until Dave Cameron was hired as head coach and GM that the team became a stable franchise and saw on-ice success. The beat was competitive then, with the *Star* and the *Sun* along with the Canadian Press covering the OHL on a regular basis. Cameron and his teams would always be fun to cover. He was a straight shooter who had a very good sense of humour once he got comfortable around you. Sometimes when you're in the media, people tell you what they think you want to hear, and Cameron wasn't like that. His teams were talented, not very flashy, but hardworking.

He always seemed to assemble a cast of characters. At one point Cameron had a Czech import player named Frantisek Lukes, who was known as "Franky" around the rink. The Majors also had an excellent goaltending tandem in Peter Budaj, who was from Slovakia, and Andy Chiodo. Whenever reporters needed to talk to Lukes, we would also ask for Budaj, who would serve as translator. Lukes was a good player so we would talk to him via Budaj quite a bit. One day near the end of the season, we once again needed an interview and translator. We waited and waited. We conducted interviews in a room that had a door leading into the Majors' dressing room. We called it "the boiler room" because it housed pipes and machines and was always so hot and muggy.

"Hey, is there a team meeting? Are Franky and Budaj coming out?" I asked their PR guy.

"No. No team meeting. I'm not sure what's keeping them," was the response.

Finally, Budaj burst through the door, looked right at us, and yelled: "Franky speaks English!"

Then he turned around and walked back out.

Franky's English wasn't great, but it was good enough for print, and we never asked for a translator again. Covering junior hockey you get to meet many players, like Budaj, who go on to pro careers and play in the NHL, but no matter how big they get it's always little stories like these I remember about them.

There are many players who don't go on to NHL careers and you remember them, too. One such player was Derek Campbell, who played for the Kingston Frontenacs. In 2001, I wrote a story headlined "Racial Slur Allegation No Shock to OHLer" in which Campbell, who was one of the few Black players in the league at the time, spoke about the kind of racism he had endured, which included being called the N-word. The league knew about that specific incident and a gross misconduct (which carried a two-game suspension) was assessed. But no one, not the offender or anyone from the offending team, or the league, called to apologize or offer support. It's been two decades since, and I'll never forget the hurt in his voice. The interview affected me greatly and I still think about it today, especially in light of the game now.

Fortunately, I had great editors at the *Star* who would never shy away from these types of stories and I was able to write several about racism in the OHL, particularly when John Vanbiesbrouck was caught using the N-word in reference to his own player on the Soo Greyhounds, Trevor Daley. I was equally fortunate to have a fantastic boss in Steve McAllister who lured me away from the *Star* in 2010 to write about the Canadian Hockey League full-time for *Yahoo Sports.* We had the most incredible pool of writers from coast to coast in all three leagues and it was the best and most comprehensive coverage for junior hockey fans.

In my first year with *Yahoo,* I went to the world hockey summit and attended a presentation by Slava Lener, who was the director of Czech national teams, where he discussed how the Canadian Hockey League's import draft was hurting development in the Czech Republic and Slovakia. That piqued my interest and writing about how the import draft works and the way other countries develop their hockey players became a pet project, one I would carry over to my work at *The Athletic.*

McAllister allowed me to travel the globe to attend several World Junior Championships, writing about a tournament that has become entwined with Canadian identity. Even hockey fans who have never watched a CHL game are glued to the action come Boxing Day. Travelling to those tournaments was the only time I'd get to use my EU passport for work, which I always found funny: an immigrant with Indian parents, using her British passport, heading to Russia or Sweden or wherever to write about hockey in Canada.

My dad passed away in 2022 and it's hard to convey how much of an impact he had on my life. He was kind and patient, and there's no way I would have pursued this career without his love, support, and passion for sports. At his funeral, one of his co-workers told me how my dad would show everyone in the office my byline in the newspaper. We miss him dearly.

14

We Can Do Hard Things

Kim McCullough

I went into labor when I was behind the bench coaching at the provincial championships. The contractions started during the second period. Nothing too bad—it was my second child so I had some idea of what I was about to go through. Normally I am pretty animated when coaching, standing on the bench with my foot on the boards, lunging forward in the way my college coach did back in the day. And this particular game warranted that animation. Both teams finished in the top six of the twenty-team Provincial Women's Hockey League, the highest level of girls hockey in the world for that age group. It was a back-and-forth high-flying affair that ended in a tightly contested 2–2 tie.

But instead of being foot up on the boards, adrenaline pumping higher and higher with every big save and missed scoring chance, I was standing arms crossed, leaning against the wall behind me, enjoying watching my team play at the peak level of performance, knowing full well that it would be the last game I would coach that season. The final buzzer sounded and I went into the dressing room to do the post-game wrap-up of our performance and discuss keys to success for our game the next morning, knowing that I wouldn't be there.

I walked out the front door of the rink, said goodbye to all the parents and fans on my way out, and met my husband and father out by the car. I told them we would be going to the hospital instead of home. I texted my assistant coaches a few hours later to let them know they'd be running the show for the rest of the tournament. I emailed the players and families at two a.m. to let them know why I wouldn't be at the rink the next day. My eldest daughter, Sasha, was born that night. I think she's going to be a hockey player.

•   •   •

I first started playing organized hockey at the age of thirteen. I grew up in downtown Toronto, across the street from a park with an outdoor rink. Still, I never really played despite being less than a hundred meters from the ice.

I was always one of the best athletes at my school and I took quickly to any sport that was thrown in front of me. I had played soccer with the boys since the age of five. If my school offered it, or the boys were playing it at the park across the street, I was in. Back then you would have called me a tomboy. I finally took up hockey at thirteen when another girl joined my all-boys soccer team. I was so excited to have her on the team with me all year around, but she left during the winter season to play hockey. That sparked an interest in me for the sport, and you could say the rest is history. When I took up hockey as a teenager, when I finally started playing, I wasn't exactly a rock star—I'd barely ever skated—but I was determined to get better and be the best and as fast as I possibly could. Being bad at a sport was not something I was okay with.

I started playing house league and went over to that outdoor rink constantly to accelerate my learning. I made a AA rep team the following year (which is the highest level of competitive hockey offered here in Ontario). Let's not pretend I skyrocketed from my humble house league beginnings to the top of the rep team in one season, though. Honestly, the only reason I even made it onto that team early on was because my friend's dad was the head coach. So when I decided two years later, at the age of fifteen, that I wanted to play college hockey at an Ivy League university, it was understandable that people thought I was crazy. I still loved playing soccer and basketball at the highest levels, but something about hockey was different. It became an all-consuming passion very quickly. My friends would be going to the movies on a Friday night and I'd be at the outdoor rink freezing my toes off practicing shot after shot by myself. To say I loved it would be a huge understatement—I was obsessed. And as luck would have it, my head coach from the ages fifteen to eighteen was the former head coach of the University of Toronto women's hockey team. He helped me believe it was possible that I could play and excel at that level.

This was back in the mid-nineties, before women's hockey was in the Olympics, and before you could just google things like "how do I play women's hockey in university." I didn't personally know anyone who'd played university hockey and had no rational reason to believe that I'd be even close to good enough to get there. But through a ridiculous amount of focus, determination, and hard work, I was able to realize my dream three short years later—after having only played the game for five years.

I absolutely had an underdog mentality throughout my entire hockey career and definitely suffered from imposter syndrome all the way through my college years. I was always worried someone would discover I wasn't really that good after all, so I looked for ways to get ahead that weren't tied to on-ice skills. I knew those would come over time (and not too long of a time given how often I was at the outdoor rink). I didn't know any other players who did hockey-specific off-ice workouts back then and certainly no one who focused on their nutrition or mental game. I believe my willingness to focus on being the best athlete possible physically and mentally contributed as much to my success on the ice as my obsession with doing the extra work at the outdoor rink. I never thought of it as a sacrifice—it was a choice I gladly made because I knew I only had a small window of time to reach my goals and I was more than willing to do whatever it took to get there.

Exactly ten years after I started my college hockey career in the Ivy League and three months after finishing my professional hockey career, I decided that I would start my own company, Total Female Hockey. I wanted to make my full-time living pursuing my true passion of empowering young female hockey players with the information and inspiration they need to drive their own success on and off the ice. I wanted to fill the massive void that had existed for me as a young player. I was desperate for any information I could get my hands on about how to train off the ice, what to eat in order to perform my best on the ice, or to go to a hockey camp with other like-minded girls who wanted to be their best. Back when I was growing up, the only training info out there at the library (pre-internet, remember?) was how to body-build in order to be a two-hundred-pound player who can throw her weight around in the corners (not really necessary or desired in the female game). The only female-specific nutrition information I could find came from magazines like *Shape*, which weren't exactly geared towards aspiring young athletes who were burning thousands of calories a day running from practice to practice to game.

I created my first off-ice training products and wrote every blog post for Total Female Hockey with the young version of me in mind. Every young version of Kim out there, desperate for the information and inspiration they needed to drive their own success, was the target audience. Again, many people told me I was crazy. It was smack dab in the middle of the recession back in 2008—not great timing. Not to mention the fact that I was creating a brand-new business model in a tiny niche market focusing entirely on female hockey. But again, two years after starting from scratch and working just as hard as I did back when I set that goal of playing university hockey when I could barely play the game, I was able to build a successful company that I've now been running for fifteen years. I do what I love, love what I do, and am able to live the life I want as a result.

Let's just say I've never exactly done things the easy way on or off the ice. And the truth is that I never really doubted that I would achieve either of those big goals on and off the ice. I must be blessed with the perfect mixture of stubbornness and confidence. Don't get me wrong, there were many points along the way where I doubted myself and found myself mentally, physically, and emotionally exhausted en route to those goals. Going from house league to playing university hockey in five years is not common and it certainly wasn't easy. Starting a brand-new business during a recession that relied on online marketing and delivery back when people were still reluctant to use their credit card online wasn't easy either. But I never gave up, even when everyone around me thought I was too obsessed and too driven (is there such a thing?). I know without a shadow of a doubt that I am doing *exactly* what I was meant to be doing in this life—and it has been my experiences within women's hockey for the past thirty years that have allowed me to realize my dreams.

I'm very fortunate to have had the opportunity to play at the highest levels of women's hockey for over a decade, coach thousands of teams and players on and off the ice, and help countless members of the female hockey community take their performance to the next level. Empowering those players, coaches, and teams with the tools they need to succeed on and off the ice, watching them challenge their limits and rise up to the challenge, whether they're new to the game or vying for a spot in the upper echelons of our sport, is what keeps my fire burning as a coach and mentor. I didn't have access to any of these types of resources or opportunities as I was coming up in our game, and now I get to share my experience and expertise with the whole hockey world. There's nothing like hearing from a young player who has worked with you on the ice all summer that she made her first-ever rep team or talking to a coach who used your training manuals and videos to take their team from a group of good players to a well-oiled machine that won the provincial championship. I get emails almost daily from all over the women's hockey world thanking me for helping them take their game to the next level and achieve their goals on the ice, but by far the greatest accomplishment I've had so far in this game is having players I've coached since they were twelve and thirteen years old give back to the game they love as coaches.

Back when I first started TFH, I set some pretty lofty goals. One of those was to inspire more female players to get into coaching and mentor them along their new hockey journey. When I wrote that goal down back in 2008, I was fresh out of playing pro hockey, had never coached a single game behind the bench, and had only been a part-time on-ice instructor at summer hockey camps between college hockey seasons. At that time, I only offered one female hockey-player-specific off-ice training manual and trained a handful of teams off the ice in the gym. So while inspiring and mentoring other female coaches is a massive part of what I do now, it seemed very pie in the sky back then. But for some reason I wrote it down anyway, and as you may have now figured out from my previous tales of extreme stubbornness and relentless work ethic, this was a goal I was not going to leave unmet.

The three coaches who really stick out in my mind when I think about my coach-mentoring role were all students at the PEAC School for Elite Athletes in Toronto where I was the girls hockey director for five years (it's also where Connor McDavid went to school before he headed off to the OHL). When I first got to PEAC, there were only two girls hockey players in the whole school, and we had thirty girls by the time I left to have my first child five years later. We skated before school four days a week and did workouts, video sessions, and mental-performance training at lunchtime or after school. As a coach who loves all aspects of player development both on and off the ice, I was in heaven.

I did all the recruiting, all the programming, and all the instructing and I loved every second of it. All of these players also played on their own club teams over and above what they did with me at PEAC, and as a result of all of this tailor-made training, each and every one of them became significantly better players very quickly. They also became quite the close-knit group of players despite some being twelve years old and some being eighteen. For the most part, the only girls in the school (which offered other sports than hockey but whose enrolment was close to 80 percent hockey players at the time) and so they all became fast friends. The older players quickly became leaders and mentors and the younger ones were challenged to keep up and close the gap every day.

Kat, Kandice, and Melissa were all a part of the building and rising of that program at PEAC and all became accomplished young female hockey coaches just a short ten years after they walked through those doors at PEAC. Like me, they played college and pro hockey. They worked at my hockey schools while in high school and university. And once they were done playing at university, they all got into coaching. Not coincidentally, they all coach at the association where I am now the head of player and coach development. We've coached together at so many camps, practices, games, and tournaments that we barely need to say a word to each other to change the drill, the lineup, or the vibe in the dressing room. They knew me back when I was just trying to get TFH off the ground, just as they were starting their journey towards their goal of playing university hockey. They were all at my wedding and my three kids all love them. They are a part of my family and I am proud to call them all my friends and colleagues. I am their role model and they are my greatest success in coaching.

I was back on the bench coaching two days after giving birth to my third child. After reading the first few paragraphs of my story, I'm sure this comes as no surprise. No one was making me get back to it that quickly, but no one was going to keep me off that bench either. By this time I'd been coaching junior hockey for four years and we were having our best season in team history. We were in the top four after the regular season, had the second- and fifth-leading scorers in the league, and the goalie with the second-best GAA and save percentage in the league. We had depth, balance, and confidence that we could make a run deep into the playoffs. Five days before I went into labor with child number three, we won our first playoff series in the history of our still young program. As luck would have it, I managed to go into labor before the start of our next series, so if everything went smoothly, I'd be back on the bench for game 1. My youngest was born on March 7 and game 1 was on March 9. We had one night at home with our newborn before hitting the road the next day to play the first game of the best-of-five series.

For those of you who have had a kid, I fully recognize that this is not a normal post-birth game plan. I've tried very hard not to be normal for most of my life, so I did what felt right for me on this one. One moment in particular will always stick out for me from game 1 of this series. Once we got to the visiting team's rink, the players got settled in the room and my husband and I made our way through the sea of parents and fans offering us their congratulations on our newest team member (while undoubtedly thinking, Kim is even crazier than we already thought). I brought my youngest into the room to meet the girls briefly before we all needed to start the pregame routine. The girls headed off to do their warm-up while my assistants and I went over the game plan and made any last-minute adjustments and relayed messages to the team. When the newborn cried, I fed her. Strangely, it felt completely normal somehow. I was stressed neither about the game nor about the baby. Right before we headed out for the first two periods (they only flooded the ice between the second and third periods in our games), I fed her one more time, my husband took the baby, and our team took to the ice.

The girls were *flying* from the first drop of the puck. Who knew that all you had to do is pop out a baby before starting a playoff series to get the team going! Now I'm not going to lie to you and say that I remember much of what happened in the game. I can tell you that despite my high levels of pure exhaustion, I felt like all of us were in a pure flow state. Passes were perfectly timed and weighted. Changes were crisp and perfectly timed. Execution was on point and intensity was through the roof and as a result, we were up by a few after the first two periods.

As we headed off the ice and back to the dressing room for the fifteen-minute flood break, I instantly flipped back over to mom mode. The baby was clearly hungry, screaming her tiny little lungs out, so it was time to feed her. The players went in their room and I went to the coaches' room to do my other job. And quite honestly, the previous five years of my life had constantly felt like this: hockey, kids, hockey, kids. Sometimes one took priority over the other. There was rarely (never) balance or a feeling of complete control. They just merged into each other constantly. Without the support of my husband and my dad, this would not have been possible. My kids were underfoot at every game, running around every rink in Ontario like they owned the place, and they were crying, laughing, and causing chaos in the background of almost every recruiting call, email, and practice plan I made for five years straight. It was what it was and it sure wasn't easy.

Which brings me back to that moment between the second and third periods. There I was feeding the thirty-six-hour-old baby, and my assistants came into the coaching room to ask what I wanted them to talk about before the team headed back out on the ice. It was great of them to ask but either of them could have easily run the show as they both had head-coaching experience.

I thought about it for a minute and then I said something along the lines of, "Let's go do it together." So I walked back into that dressing room with a blanket draped over my shoulder and baby and gave the between-periods speech to the team while breastfeeding my newborn. While that was certainly a unique experience for everyone in that room, what really stood out to me about that moment is that the players all looked right at me, locked into game mode, and were ready to go back out there and make a statement with a convincing W in game 1. Only one player was uncomfortable with me breastfeeding and she put up her hand and said, "Kim, I'm not trying to be rude but I'm just a little uncomfortable so I'm going to look down at the ground instead of at you." We had a little laugh and kept plowing through the key points before heading back out the door and onto the ice.

When I think back on that day—the long drive to the rink, the hectic pregame, the way the girls dominated from start to finish, and the joy of bringing the new member of my home team to meet my hockey team—what really stands out to me as someone who has been fully immersed in the world of women's hockey for thirty-plus years is that moment in between periods. Back when I was fifteen, sixteen, seventeen years old, I couldn't have imagined having a coach come in the room to give an in-game talk while breastfeeding. I'm not sure I could have remained as focused and poised as my players did in that moment. While I'll never really know what was going through all their teenage minds when I walked through that door, I do know that somehow I'd made bringing your family with you into the rink (no matter where and when) more normal.

I have always seen myself as a role model for players ever since I started playing college hockey back in the late nineties. And I take that role very seriously. I want every player I work with to know that they can do both: they can love their work and love their family and if they want, they, too, can do the crazy dance of running a business, coaching a sport, and having three kids at home. I want them to know that it *is* possible. It may not be common, and at times it isn't the healthiest to try to burn a candle at three ends for eight straight months of the year during hockey season. But maybe one day they'll find themselves in those moments of overwhelming craziness and think, "Kim did it, so I can do it, too."

.   .   .

I started playing organized hockey at the age of thirteen, but I became a real hockey player the year before out on the outdoor rink. When the hockey bug bit me, I became more than just a regular at that outdoor rink across from my house. I was there every chance I could get, for shinny, for open skating, for when the rink guy would let me on early or late when no one else was around. I can say for certain that the time I spent on that outdoor rink is what made me a real hockey player. Back then, they split up shinny times based on age. There was an under-12 group, a 12-to-18 group, and adult shinny. That first winter, I started with the U12 group because I knew if I went to the 12-to-18 group, I would be a human pylon. I figured I needed to play with my peers in terms of ability even if that meant being the oldest on the ice and getting dangled by an eight-year-old or two. So out I went with the youngest group, watching, learning, skating, falling, and trying to mimic what I'd seen out on TV out on the ice.

Playing shinny on the ODR (outdoor rink) was challenging (and wonderful) for a few reasons. First and foremost, you may not know anyone out there and you were for sure the only girl. I can say that in the six years that I made that ODR my home every winter, there was another girl out there less than one percent of the time. I'd grown up playing sports with the boys (and faring quite well) so this didn't bother me one bit. In fact, I'm not sure that I even thought about it as being good or bad back then. It was what it was and I simply wanted to get better by whatever means necessary. Another big challenge with shinny is that you don't have uniforms and you don't necessarily know your teammates. This means you have to remember who is actually on your team out there among the sea of hooded sweatshirts and toques. And when you wanted to pass to them or get a pass from them, you couldn't always use their name because even if they told it to you, you were never really quite sure if you were using the right name for the right person in the moment. I truly believe that playing hockey with a random group of people without matching uniforms or knowing each other's names, mixed with not really playing positions or knowing how each other play, is a great recipe for developing hockey IQ. You had to really pay attention and be proactive if you wanted to be successful on the ODR. This wasn't an environment for shrinking violets who didn't want to call for the puck or steal it from someone you'd never really met.

For the first little while on the ODR, I was a passenger, not a driver. I'd skate around with those young kids, be involved with the play without ever really making a true impact on the results and generally be fine, but not good. In addition to those almost daily shinny games, I'd be out there on my own working on my skills. There were a lot of open ice times on that little rink as it was tucked away inside a neighbourhood and it didn't get a lot of foot traffic beyond the after-school, evening, and weekend hours. So I'd go there before school or rush home after school and the rink guard would let me on as long as I promised to shovel it for him.

I loved being out there on my own. I started making up little drills for myself to work on skating, shooting, and passing. One of my all-time favourites that I still use today with the players I work with is puck-to-puck passing. You have two pucks and you shoot one out into the open ice. You then try to pass the second puck so that it hits the first puck. And you repeat, repeat, repeat. It's like playing pool or billiards out on the ice. As you can imagine, when I first started playing around with this drill, I was doing a lot of puck chasing and not having a very high success rate. But over the weeks, my passing accuracy went through the roof.

And soon I started to challenge myself even more by adding things in like making all the passes while I was moving, or passing the puck without stick-handling it first, and eventually using my backhand to make the pass. As I moved up into the higher levels of hockey, I was always an excellent passer. And the hours and hours I spent with this drill, and other drills like it, honing my craft, was why. Nowadays, a lot of players only work on their skills in a highly structured environment with a skills coach running them through drills. While there is nothing wrong with working on skills in this way, it doesn't promote creativity or problem-solving in the same way as free unstructured play does.

Which brings me back to those shinny games. After a month or so with the U12 crew, I decided I had to go play with the twelve-to-eighteen-year-olds. I had watched them play after I got off the ice with the young kids and I started to believe that I could keep up. I wasn't under any delusions of grandeur but I figured I wouldn't be the worst one out there. But I definitely was. Those first few games were brutal. I could tell that those boys didn't want me out there and definitely didn't want to see my stick picked out of the pile and thrown to their side when the teams were made. I knew a lot of them from school and knew they all played high-level rep hockey. I don't blame them for not wanting the house league girl on their team.

Luckily for me, I always had more confidence than I should have and hated to be bad at anything, especially since I played all the other sports with these same boys off the ice and was always in the top third. I just knew I wasn't going to stay at the bottom for long, so I had to figure out how to dig out of the hole.

I distinctly remember walking to the rink one day and setting a simple goal for myself: touch the puck ten times today. Given my lack of ability, no one out there was going to willingly pass me the puck. So I had to get it for myself. I had to create turnovers and steal it for myself. I learned how to use my stick to take away passing lanes, to get stick on puck while angling the player off, and how to do an effective stick lift. And I started stealing a lot of pucks (and pissing off a lot of my classmates as a result). Now that I had the little black thing, I could start using my ever-developing passing skills to distribute it. This sure made me more popular with my teammates, as I had no desire to carry it end to end and try to deke out the whole team as many of them did. I was being a good teammate—get it and give it. I started to figure out how give-and-gos worked, so I would pass it, jump into open space, and ask for it back. And slowly but surely, they started to give it back to me. Not every time, but enough that it made me think I was starting to be a bit more welcome out there.

The boys no longer made faces of disappointment when my stick was thrown on their side while picking teams. They started to pass me the puck more often because I was open and I was getting pretty good. The goals I set for myself as I walked to the rink changed accordingly. I was thinking about scoring goals and stopping one-on-ones now. I saw patterns in the play and knew when to move the puck and when to keep it. I became one of the guys. I knew their names and they knew mine, and while it still took a few years for them to want me on their team, I had made some significant leaps in the right direction. Without coaching, without cones, without drills, and without any feedback other than my own. I'd set the goals, I'd reach the goals, and I'd push myself relentlessly to get better every day. It's no mystery how I went from a house league player at twelve to a rep player at thirteen—I did the damn work when no one else was watching. And that's still how I get better as a coach, teacher, and mentor today. Relentless work ethic even when it's hard. Especially when it's hard.

I was converted from a defenceman to a forward after my first-ever skate for the Dartmouth College women's hockey team. We had a captain's practice that day, which amounted to a few warm-up drills followed by a scrimmage. The coaches watched from the press box at the top of the rink, as they weren't allowed on the ice yet due to Ivy League rules. After the skate, the coaches asked to see me in their office, which was more than a little daunting for a freshman. I went in, sat down, and was told that they wanted me to play forward instead of D. My first thought was, *I've never played a shift of forward in my whole life.* I frankly don't remember any other words that came out of their mouths after that. I just remember leaving and thinking, *I guess I have to figure out how to play forward.* For every practice, shift, and game of minor hockey, I was a D. A rushing D, mind you, who played a bit like the Tasmanian Devil, touching every corner of the ice on every shift. My effectiveness wasn't based on my adherence to structure, it was based on my ability to read the play, make a decision, and recover quickly. So it is completely understandable that my college coaches would watch me fly around the ice unbridled during that first scrimmage and think winger instead of D. I had the mindset, game set, and aggressiveness needed to be a great power forward. And that's exactly what I became—eventually. But first I had to start out on the fourth line.

I found out very quickly that I was going to find my success as a forward in the same way I started making an impact on the outdoor rink six years earlier. I was going to have to go get the puck myself. I loved hunting players down and stealing pucks on the forecheck. It became my special gift and is still one of my favourite things to coach almost thirty years later. Angling, steering, getting stick on puck, body on body and taking that puck like a thief in the night—it may not make the highlight reels but it sure makes a huge impact on the game. So how did I become so good on the forecheck? I used what I knew from playing D. The things that I hated having done to me when I played defence—having no time, having no space, feeling the forechecker breathing down my neck no matter where I turned—I perfected as a forward.

I turned forechecking into a bit of an art and it was the catalyst that took me from the fourth line to the second line before Christmas of my freshman year. I started off creating turnovers all over the ice. That earned me penalty kill time. Then I started making strong passes to my teammates off recovering those turnovers, which earned me my fair share of assists. That started to move me up the ladder on the lineup and got me more ice time. That ability to relentlessly pressure the other team's Ds, and an eagerness (quite frankly excitement) to go into the dirty areas and come out with the puck, also led to me scoring a lot of goals. They weren't always pretty. Let's be honest, they were mostly gritty. Of the fifty or so goals I scored in my four seasons in college hockey, I'd bet forty were of the ugly variety and ten might be considered nice. I sure wasn't making any highlight reels with the majority of them, but the last time I checked, all goals count equally on the scoreboard, whether you scored them off a backhand toe drag or off a greasy rebound. I always tell my players, there isn't a video of your goal on the scoresheet, it just says "goal."

I made a whole career off scoring goals from in-tight, with opponents draped all over me, on the edge of getting a goalie interference penalty (I had my fair share, no doubt). And I loved every second of it. I wasn't a slow-it-down type of player, I was a speed-it-up kind of player who loved creating chaos out on the ice. And I had just enough skill and smarts to make good things happen as a result of that chaos.

That mentality, physicality, and relentlessness is still as rare in our game now as it was back then. And it's still as effective if you harness it properly.

I finished my first season at Dartmouth with 27 points—not bad for a converted D who started the season on the fourth line. And that performance earned me my first-ever invite to a Team Canada try-out. I still find my ascension up the ranks a little hard to believe. I'll never forget when my college coach told me I was going to the camp in Montreal and I called my parents to let them know. I'd earned it, but it was still a little out there given that I'd only started playing organized hockey seven years earlier. While I scored quite a few goals at the camp, I really had no shot at making the team. I was surrounded by past, current, and future Olympians, and was lucky enough to be on a line with two of them for the tryouts. When you're playing the wing with Jennifer Botterill and Tammy Shewchuk, two of the greatest scorers and playmakers of all time who scored hundreds of goals for our archrivals at Harvard, potting a few goals at camp isn't hard. I just went to the net with my stick on the ice and good things happened. Gritty, not pretty, but still a goal in any game.

After a very successful college hockey career where we won multiple Ivy League and ECAC championships and played in two national championships, I returned home to play professional hockey in what was the original version of the NWHL, the National Women's Hockey League. No million-dollar contracts or private jets mind you, just a bunch of super-talented and highly motivated women playing at the highest level in the world without the compensation we wanted or the publicity we deserved. That never influenced how hard we worked or competed to be our best, though. We had jobs outside the rink so that we could pay our bills. Some like me pursued master's degrees to continue our education. Some had families to take care of. And we did

WE CAN DO HARD THINGS

it all while practicing late at night, training when we could, and travelling all over the province and country to play the game we loved at the highest level in the world.

The league was full of Olympians from both sides of the border, and on my first pro team, the Brampton Thunder, we had quite a few of them. Watching the all-Olympian line of Jayna Hefford, Vicky Sunohara, and Lori Dupuis dominate in every practice and every game was a sight to behold. I would still rank them as one of the most effective and well-rounded lines in the history of our game. Our lineup that year was chockful of national team players and recently graduated college hockey all-stars. We had depth, youth, and experience all wrapped into one, which led to us winning the provincial championships and finishing second at the national championship.

That first season of pro, I did what became my calling card for all six seasons at that level. I started the season as a forward and ended it as a D. My experience playing both positions made me quite versatile and led to more ice time and more opportunities. Young players often question themselves and their coaches when they are asked to switch positions, but the truth is that it should be seen as a compliment, a show of trust, and will serve them well as they move up in hockey.

I think that first year of pro was the best I ever played. I was in the best shape of my life. I had phenomenal teammates and I was being asked to play in all situations in multiple positions. This led to me being asked to move to Calgary to play with the program out of the Olympic Oval, which was called the Oval X-Treme. While it wasn't the home of the national team program per se, my teammates the next season were 90 percent from the 2002 Olympic team. Wickenheiser, Goyette, Campbell—you name it, they were there. There were a handful of players like me who had played college hockey and a bit of pro and some young kids who would eventually go on to the national team level. We trained full time, which was something new for me, and I loved every second of it.

Some days we had two ice times and a workout all in one day. That meant multiple warm-up and cool-down sessions, meals crammed in between sessions, and often an inability to move/function when you dragged yourself home at night. We did fitness testing more than any human would want to, trained hard constantly, and dominated most games we played. As someone who loved training and practicing as much as they loved the games, this was heaven for me. As I look back on it now, I know that this full-time training is the dream of all the players currently fighting for a viable professional women's hockey league here in North America.

In 2007, my final year of professional hockey, I helped found the now defunct Canadian Women's Hockey League, alongside other players such as Jayna Hefford, Sami Jo Small, Jennifer Botterill, Lisa-Marie Breton, Allyson Fox, and Kathleen Kauth. We created a centrally funded league that would be responsible for all travel, ice, uniforms, and equipment, but could not pay the players. While the journey of the professional women's hockey game in North America could best be described as tumultuous since that time, the start of the newly minted Professional Women's Hockey League in January 2024 certainly has all of us in the female hockey community excited and hopeful for the future. That has changed somewhat, but being paid a livable wage while playing professional hockey is still not a reality in our sport.

I hope that the players I coach and my two young daughters continue to have the opportunity to pursue a full-time career in female hockey. The passion, talent, and drive to make it happen has made what was once a dream, a reality. The amazing women who play at the top levels of our sport deserve to be paid and celebrated for all their awesomeness on and off the ice. They are the ultimate role models.

They are elite athletes, they are university graduates, they are small-business owners, they are mothers, they are working, going to school, making ends meet, and fighting for what they believe is not only possible but well deserved.

I would be thrilled to see my kids grow up to be like any of the amazing women I had the privilege of playing with in my six seasons of pro hockey. They already look up to all the hockey girls I coach today and think it's cool that I played with and coached so many of the players, coaches, announcers, and leaders in the female game today. All three of my kids have asked me the same question when they were about three years old: "Mommy, do boys play hockey too?" It always makes me smile and makes me even more driven to grow our game in any way I can on and off the ice from players to coaches at the grassroots level to pro all over the world. I've ended every email I've sent since I started Total Female Hockey back in 2008 with the same phrase, "Work Hard. Dream BIG." It's all I've ever known and done and all I've ever asked from the players, coaches, and families I've worked with. Always dream big, put in the work, and great things can happen for you and for our game.

15

The Logan Boulet Effect

Boulet Family

*T*he date April 6, 2018, still sends chills down the spine of hockey
fans across Canada and around the world. That was the day that
the Humboldt Broncos junior hockey team were involved in a devastating bus crash as they were on their way to a playoff game in Nipawin,
Saskatchewan. In the aftermath, sixteen people were dead and another

thirteen were injured after the Broncos' bus was destroyed by a tractor-trailer that had run a stop sign. Out of the tragedy of that fateful day, a gift emerged that keeps on giving to this day. That gift was Humboldt Broncos defenceman Logan Boulet. Logan's decision to sign his organ donation card saved six lives when he died on April 7. What nobody could have known that day was that Logan's supreme act of selflessness would go on to save thousands of lives after his passing. It is a phenomenon that is called the Logan Boulet Effect. Logan's parents, Toby and Bernie, and his sister, Mariko, are some of the most incredible human beings I have ever had the privilege of speaking with. In their own words, this is the story of a proud Humboldt Bronco and a young man who just wanted to help others, Logan Boulet.

Toby Boulet

Logan and I would sit out on our back deck in Lethbridge, Alberta, a lot. We would sit there in our chairs and hang out and talk. Logan's off-season trainer while playing in Humboldt, Ric Suggitt, passed away from a cerebral brain hemorrhage in June 2017. We were shaken up by Ric's passing. In August of that year, we were sitting on the back deck like we always do, and Logan turned to me and said, "I am going to be an organ donor like Ric." He went on, "If he can help six people after he passed away, so can I." I said, "Okay, but nobody is going to want your organs when you are eighty-five years old." Logan was insistent. I didn't even tell my wife, Bernie.

Bernie Boulet

Logan would always take his time and observe things before he tried something new.

The fact he became an organ donor is quite ironic. He wasn't always brave growing up. Logan was afraid of snakes. If Logan were about to do something he wasn't sure about, he would get giggly, that kind of nervous laugh.

Mariko Boulet

When I was in grade twelve, Logan was in grade nine and we both went to the same high school. I would drive us to school and one day we were on our way and Logan started to freak out. He was screaming and I said, "What happened?" Logan lost it, "There's a moth in the car. We need to pull over right now!" We pulled over and rolled down the window with the old-school hand crank and got the moth out of the car. He was so rattled by this little moth. Logan didn't like bugs and snakes and little animals.

One year our family went to Whistler, BC, and went zip-lining. We were all so brave and having so much fun, except for Logan. Logan was wearing this giant yellow poncho, and he was hanging on for dear life. At the end of the tour, we were all given the chance to ride the final zip-line hanging upside down! Everyone on the tour tried it out, except for Logan. His big daredevil move was to let go and go "hands-free" for a whole two seconds.

Bernie

We were a family that volunteered our time and tried to give back to the community.

Our kids grew up in that environment and understood that giving back is just what you do. Logan had a gift for making people feel important.

Toby

Logan was always a team-first guy. I remember a Midget AAA hockey tournament in Kelowna. This was the last year of Midget hockey for Logan and his team. We were winning games when one of our defencemen got hurt. Then another one got hurt, so now we are down to four defencemen. Logan got a penalty in this important game, and while he was in the penalty box, he realized that he was bleeding. The coaches and trainers took him into the dressing room. And then called me in.

Logan looked at me as I walked into the dressing room and says, "I cut myself and I don't know how." It was a deep cut on his forearm and the trainer wanted to take him to the hospital. Logan said, "Can we just tape it up and I can go to the hospital after the game?" So, we took some gauze and taped it up so Logan finished the game. After, he went to the hospital and spent two hours in Emergency getting it stitched up. That was classic Logan, he would do anything for his teammates.

Bernie

We viewed Logan going away to Humboldt to play junior hockey as an experience. Your window to play junior hockey is tiny compared to the rest of your life. We wanted to him to have that experience.

Mariko

Logan always stayed true to himself and his goals. He had to overcome being cut by various teams along the way. Whenever he was cut, he would turn that negative into a positive and keep working towards his goal. Logan was always able to stay motivated and focused. He didn't play AAA until his final year of minor hockey, and he ended up being the assistant captain of the Broncos and an important member of the team.

Bernie

The day of the bus crash, we didn't actually talk to Logan. The team used to always meet up on game day at Johnny's Bistro and have breakfast. We were at our hotel in Humboldt when Logan and the team left. I looked out the window of our hotel and I could see Logan and other players leaving Johnny's for their game-day routines before heading to the rink to board the bus.

The night before the crash, when we said goodbye to Logan, I received a huge hug from him in the lobby. Toby and I looked at him and said, "We will see you after the game tomorrow night." And that was the last time we spoke to him.

Mariko

I was in Edmonton when I got the news about the bus crash, going to the University of Alberta. I was having a tough time being so far away from home, so my aunt had offered me her tickets to go see the symphony. A friend was going to go with me. The plan was I would go to her place, we would have dinner, and then head out. My last "normal" memory is going to Save-On and picking up dessert for our dinner.

The minute I walked into her house, she hugged me. At the exact moment, I got a call from my mom. I answered the phone and my mom started yelling, "Where are you?" I said, "I am at Charlotte's, why are you yelling at me?" My mom said, "There's been an accident."

By this point, Charlotte and her roommates could hear my mom yelling on the phone. I wasn't sure what she was talking about yet. Mom just said, "The bus." I was still confused, "What bus? Who is on a bus?" Then mom blurted out, "The bus, the hockey bus!"

Mom was hysterical and crying on the phone. I started crying, too, and then Mom said, "We don't know where Logan is, but the bus, it is the worst thing I have ever seen."

I was trying to gather my thoughts and figure out what to do. Charlotte and her roommates put on *The Office*, something light to watch to help calm me down. Not long afterwards my dad called and said, "We found Logan, and he is heading to a hospital." I was so overcome with happiness that they found Logan and he was heading to a hospital because that meant he was alive. But when I went to share the news with those I was with, nobody in the room shared my excitement. They all just continued to look at me with devastation on their faces.

At first, my dad said I didn't need to come to Saskatoon which was where Logan was being transported to and where they were heading. Twenty minutes later he called me back and said, "We decided that no matter what happens, we need to be together as a family." He said my cousin Kelly was going to pick me up.

Charlotte drove me home in my car, and she and her roommates helped me pack a bag. I packed everything I would need to camp out at a hospital for days, including comfy clothes and a pillow. I also packed my homework so I could study. Kelly picked me up at my place in Edmonton, and he drove me for the five hours it takes to get from Edmonton to the hospital in Saskatoon. Kelly started driving around eleven at night and we arrived in Saskatoon just after three in the morning.

My dad was calling me throughout the drive to keep me updated on what was going on. At one point, we were in the middle of nowhere in Saskatchewan and my dad told me that Logan wasn't going to make it.

Dad said, "We love you, and we will see you when you get here."

I told Kelly and he started bawling and wiping tears from his eyes. I remember Kelly passing me some tissues and swerving all over the highway. I remember wondering if I should offer to drive because he didn't seem like he would be able to. I was silently crying, almost in a state of shock. The news didn't register at first, it was too much.

Toby

The night of the bus crash, my wife and I were taken into a little room at the hospital in Saskatoon. There were four doctors and a social worker joining us. After the doctors were done explaining everything and it was obvious that Logan wasn't going to make it, my wife looked at me. The doctors had just told us that Logan would soon be "brain passed," which is what they say instead of "brain dead," like they say on TV.

I looked at the doctors and said, "Do we have to get a second opinion?" One of the doctors spoke and said, "No, this is the best group of doctors in the province." Bernie looked at me and said, "Can we donate Logan's organs?" The doctors had a stunned look on their faces after she said that. They were not ready to hear that, and Bernie didn't know that Logan had already volunteered his organs. I told them that Logan had signed his organ donation card and they said, "Okay, let's go."

Bernie said, "Logan is healthy and strong and fit, and he won't need his organs where he is going to go."

Bernie

I wasn't shocked when I found out that Logan was an organ donor because that is the kind of thing that he would do. The doctors had told us about the severity of the injury to Logan's brain stem and how he would not be able to recover from it. Logan was one of sixteen people that passed away in the Humboldt bus crash, and he was the only one where everything lined up perfectly for him to donate his organs.

Logan's official day of passing is April 7, 2018. He was declared brain passed at 11:45 a.m. the morning of the 7th. He didn't have to go into surgery to recover his organs until just before two in the morning, so we were able to get all that time with him before he was taken away. We were lucky, there were fourteen other families who didn't get that time; their loved ones had already passed. Athletic Therapist Dayna Brons held on until her passing on April 11.

His heart was beating, and he was warm; so, we talked to him and sang songs. We also read stories to him and held his hand. I cherish that time we spent with him.

The nurses at the hospital were incredibly kind and caring. Even though he was brain passed, they talked to him the whole time they were working on him. They would say, "Okay Logan, we are going to take some blood. Just so you know that is happening." Or "We are giving you a needle for a test we need." When they did the ultrasound, the technician told my brother how strong his heart was. Logan was brain passed, but he was still brave enough to pass on his heart so that someone else could live.

Toby

Later that night, as we went through the process of signing the paperwork for his organ donation, Logan's billet family showed up at the hospital. The Paulsens' son, McLaren, who was thirteen years old at the time, overheard us talking about organ donation and said, "Oh, Logan told me about that." We were stunned. McLaren said that recently they were sitting in Logan's car in front of the house, by the maple tree. McLaren asked Logan what he was going to do for his twenty-first birthday. Logan said, "I am going to sign my donor card, because my friend Ric did." The tragic bus crash took place five weeks after he signed his card.

Each province in Canada has different rules and regulations when it comes to organ donation. We didn't know that until Logan passed away. We were told that night.

Saskatchewan is the most conservative province in Canada when it comes to donation. We didn't know that until Logan passed away.

Since the crash and Logan's donations, the Saskatchewan government has made substantial changes to their policy. They now have an online organ donation registry, something they never had before.

Bernie

In the United States, you often see stories about families meeting the recipients of a loved one's organs. In Canada, it doesn't exactly work that way. Because Logan's organ recovery happened in Saskatchewan, we are under their provincial rules. We get asked all the time, "Have you met any of the recipients?" And the truth is we have not. In order to make contact, we have to write a generic and nondescript letter. We can't mention Logan passed away in the Broncos bus crash. That isn't allowed in Saskatchewan. You write a generic letter, and that letter goes to the Saskatchewan transplant association. And they read the letter to see if it meets their guidelines, and then, and only then, do they contact the organ donation organizations in the places that the recipients live. We do know there were recipients in Alberta, one in Saskatchewan, and some in Ontario. From there, they would contact the recipients and tell them that they have a letter from the donor family and do you want it. They can say yes or no.

Toby

We have received two letters from recipients. One was from a kidney transplant recipient, and one was from a heart transplant recipient. One was handwritten and the other letter was typed. They were both very generic letters.

Bernie

Anybody who received an organ from someone in the early days of April of 2018, there is a good chance that they already know where it came from. Toby and I both know a ton more about organ donation than we did before the crash. It doesn't mean we know everything, but we are learning.

In Canada, there isn't a transplant surgeon who will do a transplant if the family says no. For instance, Logan could have signed his card, and if Bernie and I had said no, then the process would have stopped right there.

Toby

Our understanding is that can happen in any province, even in Nova Scotia. Nova Scotia is one of the first places in North America that have presumed consent when it comes to organ donation.

Bernie

The other thing you have to remember is not all hospitals are able to handle organ recovery. We happened to be in Saskatoon after the bus crash and they were able to handle organ recovery. If Logan had been taken to Melfort or someplace else, they would have been forced to move him to another hospital that is capable of handling organ donation.

•   •   •

Bernie

The day of the service at the rink, a car picked us up at our house. As we arrived, the lineup of people waiting to get into the arena seemed to go on forever. The parking lot at the rink was jammed. People were forced to park a long way away and walk.

As we entered the building, there were two moms and their two sons. Both of the boys were in the class that I was teaching at the time. That meant so much to me. The funeral attendants took us into a dressing room so we could gather ourselves before the start of the service. Some friends of ours had installed these devices in the dressing room so it smelled nice, not like hockey equipment. We walked in through the players' bench, and the entire floor of the arena was filled with people and the stands were packed.

It was overwhelming. It hit me that so many people have ridden a bus at some point in their lives to attend a sporting or cultural event or to travel somewhere. I believe that was one of the reasons that Logan's death and the Humboldt bus crash impacted so many people.

We went to the cemetery afterwards for the burial, then came back to the arena. I couldn't get past the lobby, I kept meeting and talking to people, and they had come from all over the place.

Mariko

The funeral home in Lethbridge has been around for over a hundred years and they said that Logan's funeral was the biggest that they have ever done. When we were driving back from the family-only gravesite service, there were so many people still there at the arena, waiting to speak with us. Five of my friends from the University of Alberta came, too. I wasn't expecting that because it was finals week. They came down for one night and then they drove straight back to write their exams.

I will never forget that. It was such a quick trip that they didn't even have time to stop in at my parents' house or wait after the service for a quick hug.

Toby

Well over two thousand people showed up to pay their respects. One of Bernie's cousins created a memory book and invited people to write messages. There were simply too many people to speak with everyone. A young woman had written this message:

> One of the most distinct memories I have of Logan was sitting in Physics class. I was debating whether I should run for student council. Logan overheard what I was saying to my friend, and he said, "Go for it, because I believe in you."

> That was Logan for you.

Mariko

Prior to the crash, Logan was busy preparing to go to university in Lethbridge after he was done playing hockey in Humboldt. He had made a plan to start by taking a general science degree and then moving on to education. We talked a lot about university and what classes he should take.

He said to me, "You know what you are doing. And you are so organized!" I was proud that he acknowledged that.

For his birthday, I went to the University of Lethbridge bookstore when I was home during reading week and picked him out a U of L–branded clipboard and a few other school supplies that I use to be better organized. When we cleaned out Logan's room in Humboldt, I found that clipboard and there were notes on the paper, talking about his plans for the future. He was mapping out what he was going to take at university. That was very touching, and it made me burst into tears.

• • •

Bernie

After Logan's death, we discovered many people who were connected to Logan. Our daughter graduated from the University of Lethbridge in spring 2017. At the convocation, we got to talking with a family sitting behind us, who also had a daughter graduating. It turned out they were from Humboldt. What a coincidence as we told them that Logan played for the Broncos. As we talked, we learned their daughter's cousin, Owen, was there from Whitehorse, attending the ceremony, too.

He was around fourteen years old. He met Logan and they chatted about hockey. Logan was so gracious with his time.

That was the only time that Logan met Owen, at Mariko's convocation. It was just by chance that we happened to be sitting in a row, right in front of Owen's aunt and uncle.

They'd obviously shared a connection over hockey. They'd only spoken for a few minutes, but Logan had made a big impact.

After the crash, Owen got green and yellow tape for his hockey stick, in honour of the Broncos.

Owen is a good player and eventually went to Prince George to play Midget AAA hockey. The year after Logan died, Owen's Midget AAA team made the Mac's Midget AAA Tournament: a huge minor hockey tournament in Calgary. We went to go watch Owen and he came out to talk to us after one of his games.

As we spoke to him, we looked down and there was a dime on the floor. There's a tradition that if you find a dime, it means someone who has passed away is thinking about you. I picked it up and looked at Owen, "This is for you. Logan is coming to watch you play." Now that he's older, Owen has a tattoo of that dime we found there, with the words "work hard, play hard, have fun."

In my pocket, I carry around five dimes. They're always with me. I found them after Logan died. They make me feel like Logan is watching over us.

Mariko

Because it is important to my mom, whenever I find a dime, I send a picture of it to her. I spoke before about the moth-in-the-car story and how much Logan hated moths. After Logan's death, there was a moth that hung out on the window by our front door and wouldn't leave our house. It was green. I thought, *That must be Logan, letting us know he's still there.*

• • •

Toby

A gentleman named David Peckham out of Vancouver started Green Shirt Day, which, every April, brings awareness and attention to organ donation. He is an advocate and has been a champion of organ donation awareness for thirty years. David waited two months after Logan passed away before he phoned us. We respected that a lot. We were hardly cut off from the world, though. When Logan died, we never shut our front door for three months. Logan loved sunshine, so we left that door open to let light in. We also had visitors almost every single day.

We thought David was nice, but we didn't know what to think about his request to use Logan's story to help create Green Shirt Day. One of Bernie's cousins is a lawyer, and two of our friends are knowledgeable about the law. They were really helpful and gave us a list of questions we should ask David.

We sent the list to David and he called us three or four weeks later, but we were still not ready to make a decision at the time. Afterwards, as we thought about it, one of our concerns was whether or not he was trying to profit off Logan. I wasn't sure how real Green Shirt Day was and if it was really going to happen. Another concern we had, we wanted to be able to control Logan's image and his name. We wanted to make sure that David would honour our agreement and give us final edit on everything that goes out. And he does, we have final say on everything with Logan's image and likeness.

We had told him flat out, "Here's the deal: you have to be able to answer these questions. If you can, we will agree." He answered all of them and we made a deal. We have no contract with David, it is a handshake agreement.

The Green Shirt Day deal is he can only put images online of Logan that we give him. He can only post things on the webpage and media releases that we vet. David usually calls me once or twice a week. In the month of March, leading up to Green Shirt Day, he phones me once a day.

We were leery to begin with, but then we thought about Logan. He was the kind of kid that led from the back of the room, and we felt he'd approve. The first time they had a Green Shirt Day was in 2019. It honoured the Logan Boulet Effect and Humboldt Strong, and it was outstanding. We had support from every level of hockey that you can think of. The Humboldt Broncos were great and NHL teams were also supportive, and they still are. The Canadian Transplant Association along with Canadian Blood Services have been national community partners since the beginning.

There are numerous families in Canada that have contacted us and told us that their child, husband, wife, or whoever was inspired by Logan's story. They tell us that their loved one signed up as an organ donor because of what Logan did; and now that person has passed. It makes us wonder: How many lives has Logan saved?

Bernie

When we agreed to be a part of Green Shirt Day, I would have never thought how big it has become and the impact that it is making. In October 2018, when we went to the Kidney Foundation of Canada, Southern Alberta and Saskatchewan Branch, fundraiser that was held in Saskatoon, that was the first time we had really seen the impact Logan's organ donation had on people. It was overwhelming to have all these people come up to us and thank us for what Logan did. It was difficult to process at first.

Toby

After speaking about Logan, we were still trying not to cry. People just wanted to thank us for putting Logan's story out there. They would say that because of Logan, it is going to make organ donation in Canada so much better.

At first, it was too much, and we didn't want to talk to anyone about Logan. It was tough to hear about someone being saved because someone else lost their life and donated their organs. It took us almost a year to move past those strong emotions and embrace the idea of being part of an "angel donor family." We don't call them deceased donors; we call them angel donors. In a sense, we're all connected after a donation, and we like that idea.

Now we embrace our role, speaking across Canada promoting Green Shirt Day, and we're involved with the Alberta board of the Canadian Transplant Association, AlbertaORGANization Group, Alberta Transplant Institute, and educational committees with Canadian Blood Services (Organ and Tissue Donation and Transplantation), too. We annually host a fundraiser each year in Logan's name, and the money raised all goes to anything supporting organ donation, youth sports, youth fine arts, something in Humboldt, and the Logan Boulet Endowment Fund.

In 2018, there were 189 heart transplants in Canada, and one of them was Logan's. There are more people who require organs than there are donors. The medical community calls them "missed opportunities." There are too many missed opportunities every year.

There was research that showed 90 percent of Canadians support organ donation, yet just over 30 percent are registered donors. Most people Logan's age are not thinking about dying and donating organs. Most of them think they are going to live forever. And not all provinces make it easy for you to register as a donor.

In the wake of the crash, and after learning about Logan, there was a large number of Canadians who signed their organ donation card. They estimate around 150,000 people across the country became organ donors after hearing the news.

Toby

Canadian Blood Services is given the task of keeping track of organ transplants and donations in Canada. Canadian Blood Services has approximately four thousand employees, around seventy-five are involved in the Organ and Tissue Donation and Transplantation division. One of their tasks is to work with the provinces and territories to collect the organ donation and organ donor registration numbers. When Logan passed away in 2018, only six provinces in Canada had online organ donation registration. Since then, Saskatchewan and almost all provinces are all online. Because each province has different systems in place keeping track of their organ donations, it is hard to keep a completely accurate number of people who have registered to be a donor. What they do is make their best estimation of the numbers. Each year, keeping track of the number of people who have registered as donors is improving. In some provinces, we can get the number of people who registered to be a donor on a daily basis if we asked them.

The bottom line is that Canada does not have a national organ donation registry, whereas the United States does. That is another part of the issue we are facing. Because Logan was in Saskatchewan, and we were there at the time, Bernie was able to offer his organs for donation, and I supported it. This was because Logan registered in Alberta, but he wasn't registered in Saskatchewan. It was only because we were there at the hospital in Saskatoon and we both supported the organ donation that it happened. Parental support is a big issue when it comes to organ donation in Canada.

Bernie

In Canada, a parent or a spouse can override the person's wishes to be a donor. I have spoken to a number of critical care doctors, and they said that in a time of crisis, families don't always know what they can and can't do when it comes to organ donation. We continually encourage families and friends to have a conversation about donation, the Kitchen Table Talk.

Our family is very careful to point out that it is not just Logan: it was the circumstances of his death and everything that went with it.

People need to understand, there is no national organ donor registry in Canada. It was only because we were there in the hospital that night in Saskatchewan that Logan's wish to be a donor could be honoured.

Mariko

As Green Shirt Day took off, it hit me that this is a huge thing that is happening. The social media campaign around Green Shirt Day exploded. Some people that I barely speak to sent me photos they had posted on their social media, showing me how they are supporting the day. It is hard dealing with the loss of Logan, but it helps a lot that we have something to honour his memory.

I think of Green Shirt Day as a day to celebrate Logan, honour his legacy, and spread awareness for an important cause, instead of a horrible, awful day to remember.

Toby

Hockey is an amazing game where a team always has to become one to be successful. We got to attend an Ottawa Senators game one day, with our daughter and her friend. The then owner, Eugene Melnyk, had invited us. He'd had a liver transplant and was an advocate for organ donation.

After the game, we got to meet defenceman Mark Borowiecki and his wife. That was a surprise. Security said to us, "Mr. Borowiecki and his wife want to meet you." They escorted us down to the dressing room and we met his wife first. She is a beautiful person, and like my wife, she is also a schoolteacher. Mark came out and even though he needed to get treatment in the medical room, he wanted to take us on a tour first.

We got to the stick room and Mark looked as us and said, "You want a stick?"

I said, "What do you mean?"

He said, "Have a stick. Here is one for you, one for your daughter, and one for your daughter's friend. But don't tell anyone, because if the equipment guy sees that he will get mad because I give too many sticks away."

Brady Tkachuk spoke to us, too, and finally Mark went to get checked out by the medical staff. We appreciated that whole experience so much. I watched Mark and the way he played, and it reminded me of Logan. Like Mark, Logan was rough and tough and did whatever he had to in order to win.

•   •   •

Mariko

I have a tattoo of Logan's signature on my left forearm. I got the tattoo almost one month to the day of the bus crash, on May 4. Other people have got tattoos in honour of Logan. I think it is cool how much people care about Logan to do that.

Toby

Bernie and I don't have any tattoos; however, many of Logan's friends ending up getting a tattoo to honour him, well over ten. They are all gorgeous and many of them are a heart shape. One of them has a tattoo of an actual heart with the date of Logan's death and the words "The Logan Boulet Effect" written on the border.

Bernie

We love hearing stories about Logan from other people. In fall 2021, we were out with some friends, including one of Logan's friends, Jesse, who is now a high-performance trainer with the University of Lethbridge. He was telling us stories about Logan that we never knew, and we really enjoyed hearing them.

Toby

For years, before the crash, I coached rugby, and every time I went on the road I would tell Logan, "Look after Bernie and Mariko if something goes wrong." One day, he asked me to stop saying that. He was about fifteen years old, so I just stopped. To this day, I am convinced that Logan looks after us. Every time we get in a car and go for a drive, I always ask Logan to take care of us.

Mariko

After Logan died, I would journal to him as my way of talking to him. I filled an entire journal that first year with memories and simple, everyday chatter. I have vivid dreams and I often dream of Logan as an adult. One time I noticed him in my dream, in a way that didn't really make sense in regard to what else was happening, and I said, "Where did you come from?" He looked at me and said, "I have always been here." I liked that. I miss him so much.

Toby

My wife and I believe in the idea that you make something of yourself by what you give to society. Service is the rent you pay to live your life. By donating his organs, Logan gave more of himself than we ever thought possible.

Bernie

Logan was at his bravest when he was needed the most.

Toby

Logan would do anything for his teammates. That is the kind of kid he was. Team first, and always there to help others.

Acknowledgements

As with any book project that I have been privileged to be a part of, I have so many people that I have to thank.

First, I have to thank my amazing wife. I was a lost soul before I met her, and her support throughout the writing of this book was invaluable. I also must thank our two daughters and our pets for all of their support.

Thank you to the management and staff at my radio station, 105.9 The Region, for their continued support. As always, I must give special thanks to my agent, Brian Wood. Despite his questionable choice of a favourite hockey team, he is an outstanding literary agent.

Thanks to the ultimate literary all-star team, the entire staff of Simon & Schuster Canada. It takes a talented team to take the dream of a book and turn it into reality.

Special thanks to the staff at Hockey Canada, the Cincinnati Cyclones, Canadian Blind Hockey, the Windsor Spitfires, the Hockey Hall of Fame, the Ottawa Senators, the Nashville Predators, the NHL, the IIHF, Canada's National Women's Hockey team, HEROS Hockey, and SuperHEROS, the Humboldt Broncos, and everyone involved with Green Shirt Day.

During the research and the writing of the book, I relied on a variety of websites. Thank you to HockeyCanada.ca, TSN.ca, CBC.ca, CTV.ca, Globalnews.ca, TheStar.Com, SJHL.ca, HumboldtBroncos.com,

ACKNOWLEDGEMENTS

CHL.ca, GreenShirtDay.ca, IIHF.com, HHOF.com, Sportsnet.ca, ESPN.ca, ECHL.com, Hockeydb.com, HockeyReference.com, NHL.com, Olympics.com, and PostMedia.com.

I am eternally indebted to all of our contributors for being so generous with their time and their willingness to talk so openly. In no particular order, thank you to the entire Boulet family, Jim Paek, Angela James, Dean Barnes, Marian Jacko, Leonard Lye, Mark Borowiecki, Graham McWaters, Michelle Reid and her family, Jason Payne, Kelly Serbu, Rob Kerr, Leonard Lye, the hockey-loving women of Windsor, and our special contributors Sunaya Sapurji and Kim McCullough.

And a special thank-you to the man they call the Bob-Father, the one and only Bob McKenzie. Thanks, Bob. You're a good man.

About the Author

JIM LANG is a sportscaster, journalist, the bestselling author of *My Day with the Cup*, and the coauthor of hockey memoirs by Tie Domi, Max Domi, Wendel Clark, and Bryan Berard, as well as *Everyday Hockey Heroes, Volumes I* and *II* with Bob McKenzie. He hosts *The Jim Lang Show* on 105.9 The Region. He lives outside Toronto with his wife and kids.